Language Essentials for Teachers of R

Module 2

The **Speech Sounds** of **English: Phonetics, Phonology**, and **Phoneme Awareness**

Second Edition

Louisa C. Moats, Ed.D.

Presenter's Kit by Carol Tolman, Ed.D.

Sopris West®
EDUCATIONAL SERVICES

A Cambium Learning® Company

BOSTON, MA · LONGMONT, CO

Printed in the United States of America
Published and Distributed by

Sopris West®
EDUCATIONAL SERVICES

A Cambium Learning® Company

4093 Specialty Place • Longmont, Colorado 80504
(303) 651-2829 • www.sopriswest.com

(169279/340/5-08)

How does copyright pertain to LETRS® Module 2?

- It is illegal to reproduce any part of the LETRS Module 2 book in any way and for any reason without written permission from the copyright holder, Sopris West® Educational Services. This applies to copying, scanning, retyping, etc.
- It is illegal to reproduce LETRS Module 2 materials to distribute or present at a workshop without written permission from the copyright holder.
- It is illegal to use the name LETRS in association with any workshop, materials, training, publications, etc., without written permission from the copyright holder.

Dedication

To my husband, Steve Mitchell, who publishes, supports, and believes in our work.

—LCM

Acknowledgments

LETRS® modules have been developed with the help of many people. The national LETRS trainers—including Carol Tolman, Mary Dahlgren, Nancy Hennessy, Susan Hall, Marcia Davidson, Deb Glaser, Linda Farrell, Judi Dodson, Pat Sekel, Joan Sedita, Anthony Fierro, and Anne Whitney—have offered valuable suggestions for improving module content and structure. Their commitment to delivering LETRS across the country is appreciated beyond measure.

Bruce Rosow, Kevin Feldman, Susan Lowell, Patricia Mathes, Marianne Steverson, Lynn Kuhn, Jan Hasbrouck, Marsha Berger, Susan Smartt, and Nancy Eberhardt contributed their expertise to all LETRS first edition modules and often provide valuable input and feedback. Many other professionals from all over the country who have attended institutes and offered constructive criticism have enabled the continual improvement of LETRS and related materials. We hope you see your influence on all of the second edition modules.

We are grateful for the competent support of the Sopris West editorial and production staff, including Holly Bell, Jeff Dieffenbach, Michelle LaBorde, Rob Carson, Karen Butler, Sherri Rowe, Geoff Horsfall, Jill Stanko, and Kay Power. Special thanks are due to Toni Backstrom, who manages the LETRS program with enthusiasm, competence, and flare, and to Steve Mitchell, the publisher of LETRS.

About the Author

Louisa C. Moats, Ed.D., is a nationally recognized authority on reading instruction, how children learn to read, why many people have trouble reading, and treatment of reading problems. Louisa has been a neuropsychology technician, teacher, graduate school instructor, licensed psychologist, researcher, conference speaker, and author. She spent 15 years in private practice in Vermont, specializing in evaluation of and consultation with individuals of all ages who experienced difficulty with reading, spelling, writing, and oral language. After advising the California Reading Initiative for one year, Louisa was site director of the NICHD Early Interventions Project in Washington, D.C., a four-year project that included daily work with inner-city teachers and children. Recently, she has devoted herself to the improvement of teacher training and professional development.

Louisa earned her bachelor's degree at Wellesley College, her master's degree at Peabody College of Vanderbilt, and her doctorate in reading and human development from the Harvard Graduate School of Education. She was licensed to teach in three states before undertaking her doctoral work. In addition to LETRS®, Louisa has authored and coauthored books including *Speech to Print: Language Essentials for Teachers; Spelling: Development, Disability, and Instruction; Straight Talk About Reading* (with Susan Hall), *Parenting a Struggling Reader* (with Susan Hall), and *Basic Facts About Dyslexia and Other Reading Problems* (with Karen Dakin). Instructional materials include *Spellography* (with Bruce Rosow) and *Spelling by Pattern* (with Ellen Javernick and Betty Hooper).

Louisa's many journal articles, book chapters, and policy papers include the American Federation of Teachers' *Teaching Reading Is Rocket Science*, the Learning First Alliance's *Every Child Reading: A Professional Development Guide*, and Reading First's *Blueprint for Professional Development*.

Contents

Chapter 3 **Phonology and Spelling**

Chapter 4 **Understanding Language Differences**

Chapter 5 **Teaching Phonological Skills**

Chapter 6 **Assessment of Phonological Skills**

Introduction to LETRS®

LETRS® (*Language Essentials for Teachers of Reading and Spelling*) is professional development for educators who are responsible for improving K–12 instruction in reading, writing, and spelling. The content of LETRS is delivered in a series of 12 core modules in book format. Each module in the series focuses on one topic, with the topics aligned to be delivered in sequential training. Thus, one book for use in the course of training—and later as a professional reference—is provided for each module. Each module is typically delivered in a one- to two-day presentation by a national, regional, or local district trainer who has met the LETRS trainer certification guidelines developed by Dr. Moats and her colleagues.

module [mŏjūl] n.
a self-contained component of a whole that is used in conjunction with, and has a well-defined connection to, the other components

LETRS modules are used for both in-service training and for undergraduate and graduate courses in reading and literacy. They can also be resources for any educator charged with improving the language skills of students. LETRS is designed so that participants will understand:

1. *How* children learn to read and *why* some children have difficulty with this aspect of literacy;
2. *What* must be taught during reading and spelling lessons and *how to teach* most effectively;
3. *Why* all components of reading instruction are necessary and *how* they are related;
4. *How to interpret* individual differences in student achievement; and
5. *How to explain* the form and structure of English.

LETRS modules are designed to be delivered in sequence, but flexible sequencing is possible. In sequence, the modules build on overview concepts and introductory content, and then on phonology, phoneme awareness, and the writing system (orthography) of English (Modules 1–3). Next, the modules progress to topics in vocabulary, fluency, and comprehension instruction (Modules 4–6). Later modules (7–9) target reading instruction for the primary grades and include a module on assessment for prevention and early intervention. The final series (Modules 10–12), designed for educators who work with students at grade 3 and above, address advanced phonics and word study, comprehension and study skills in content-area reading, and assessment.

A presenter CD-ROM (developed by Dr. Carol Tolman) accompanies each LETRS module, providing a PowerPoint® presentation that supports, extends, and elaborates module content. The presentation slides are designed to be used by professional development personnel, higher education faculty, consultants, reading specialists, and coaches who have a strong background in the concepts and who have been trained to deliver LETRS modules.

LETRS is not a reading instruction program, and LETRS modules do not substitute for program-specific training. Rather, LETRS complements and supports the implementation of programs aligned with scientifically based reading research (SBRR). A complete approach to improving reading instruction must include: (a) selection and use of core and supplemental instructional materials; (b) professional development on how to use the materials; (c) professional development that leads to broader understandings; (d) classroom coaching and in-school supports; (e) an assessment program for data-based problem-solving; and (f) strong leadership. A comprehensive, systemic approach with these elements will support a Response to Intervention (RtI) initiative.

We recommend that teachers who have had little experience with or exposure to the science of reading and research-based practices begin with LETRS *Foundations* (Glaser & Moats, 2008). *Foundations* is a stepping stone into the regular LETRS modules. Other related resources have been developed to support LETRS professional development, including:

- LETRS Interactive CD-ROMs for Modules 2, 3, 4, 7, and 8 (developed with a grant from the Small Business Innovation Research [SBIR] program of the National Institute of Child Health and Human Development [NICHD]), which provide additional content and skill practice for topics often considered challenging to implement and teach in the classroom.
- *ParaReading: A Training Guide for Tutors* (Glaser, 2005)
- *The Reading Coach* (Hasbrouck & Denton, 2005)
- *Teaching English Language Learners: A Supplementary* LETRS *Module* (Arguelles & Baker, in press)
- *Early Childhood* LETRS (Hart Paulson, in press)
- *Teaching Reading Essentials* (Moats & Farrell, 2007), a series of video modeling used extensively by LETRS trainers throughout the delivery of training.

The chart on the next page represents a fundamental idea in LETRS—that language systems underlie reading and writing, and students' difficulties with reading and writing are most effectively addressed if the structures and functions of language are taught to them directly. We ask teachers to learn the terminology of language systems and to recognize that language is an important common denominator that links reading with writing, speaking, and listening comprehension.

Content of LETRS Modules Within the Language-Literacy Connection

Components of Comprehensive Reading Instruction	Organization of Language						
	Phonology	Morphology	Orthography	Semantics	Syntax	Discourse and Pragmatics	Etymology
Phonological Awareness	2	2					
Phonics, Spelling, and Word Study	3, 7	3, 7, 10	3, 7, 10				3, 10
Fluency	5	5	5	5	5		
Vocabulary	4	4	4	4	4		4
Text Comprehension		6		6	6	6, 11	
Written Expression			9, 11	9, 11	9, 11	9, 11	
Assessment	8, 12	8, 12	8, 12	8, 12	8, 12	8, 12	

Note: Numbers represent individual modules in the LETRS series.

Overview of Module 2

Module 2 delves into the vital topic of phonology—speech-sound processing—and its important relationship to reading, spelling, and oral language. Participants learn the speech-sound *system* (not just a list of sounds) of English. This module:

*   delineates the differences among the "ph" words (phonics, phoneme awareness, phonology, etc.);
*   explains why phoneme awareness is important and how it is acquired;
*   presents the consonant phoneme system;
*   presents the vowel phoneme system;
*   illustrates the differences between English and Spanish speech sounds;
*   interprets children's reading and spelling errors; and
*   proposes instructional practices in phonological and phoneme awareness.

Participants actively practice the production of speech sounds. They learn which sounds are confusable and how to give corrective feedback to students. Video modeling and role-play are used to practice instructional activities.

Chapter 1 Phonology and Phonological Awareness

Learner Objectives for Chapter 1

- Define and appropriately use the "phon" words.
- Respond to a range of phonological tasks.
- Know why explicit teaching of phonological skill is important.
- Understand the typical progression of phonological skill development.
- Orally segment any word by syllable, onset-rime, and phoneme.

Warm-Up: Phonological Tasks

- Let your instructor lead you through these tasks. We expect that you may be unsure of some answers.

    1. *Syllable Counting:* How many syllables are in each of the following words?

       theatrical _____   **appreciated** _____   **fishes** _____

       cleaned _____   **scarcity** _____

    2. *Rhyme Judgment:* Do each of these word pairs rhyme (yes or no)? Speakers may differ in their judgments.

       put, putt _____   **been, when** _____   **loyal, toil** _____

       merry, scary _____   **on, yawn** _____   **perk, Turk** _____

    3. *Dialect:* Pronounce each of these words. Which pronunciations might reveal your regional or ethnic origins?

       ❑ **tomato**   ❑ **parker**   ❑ **oil**   ❑ **caught**   ❑ **wash**   ❑ **sing**

    4. *Odd Word Out:* Which word does not begin with the same sound as the others?

       ❑ **theory**   ❑ **therefore**   ❑ **thistle**   ❑ **thinker**

    5. *Phoneme Matching:* Which word has the same last sound as the word **does**?

       ❑ **miss**   ❑ **nice**   ❑ **prize**   ❑ **purchase**

6. *Initial Phoneme Isolation:* Isolate and say the first speech sound in each of these names.

   Eunice _____   **Charlotte** _____   **Wyatt** _____   **Quinn** _____

7. *Phoneme Blending:* Blend these sounds together to make a whole, real word.

   /th/ /ŭ/ /m/   _____

   /m/ /or/ /f/ /ē/ /m/   _____

   /s/ /t/ /ǎ/ /k/ /s/   _____

   /y/ /ū/ /n/ /ə/ /v/ /er/ /s/   _____

8. *Phoneme Segmentation:* Raise a finger for each sound as you break each of these words into its individual speech sounds (phonemes).

   shear   _____   **chains**   _____

   quite   _____   **clutch**   _____

9. *Phoneme Deletion*
   - Say **driver**. Say it again without the /v/.   _____
   - Say **smoke**. Say it again without the /m/.   _____
   - Say **sink**. Say it again without the /ŋ/ (ng).   _____
   - Say **six**. Say it again without the /k/.   _____

10. *Phoneme Sequence Identification:* What is the <u>third</u> speech sound in each of these words?

    chunk _____   **bathe** _____   **vision** _____   **exit** _____

Phonology and Learning to Read

One of the four major brain-processing systems we studied in Module 1 is the phonological processor. It is specialized for perceiving, remembering, interpreting, and producing the speech-sound system of a person's language. The phonological processor does not process musical tones or recognize environmental sounds. It has many "jobs," but all of them are specific to **phonology** (one of the systems that language comprises). Language networks, usually in the left half of the brain, enable us to recognize, produce, and interpret speech. The term *phonological* is preferred over "auditory" when we are referring to language functions.

Figure 1.1. The Four-Part Processing Model of Word Recognition

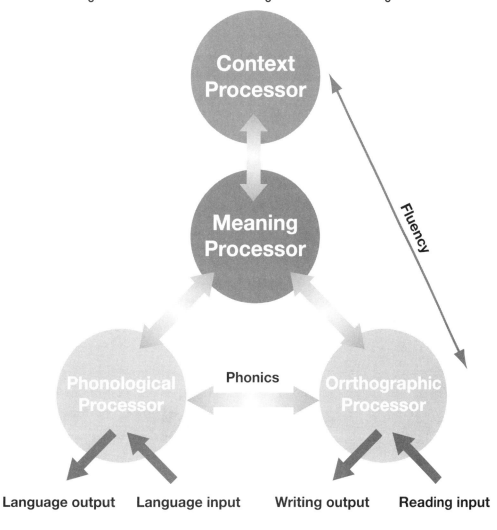

Various brain areas (e.g., context processor, meaning processor, and orthographic processor) are specialized for processing other aspects of language, including **syntax** (sentence structure), **semantics** (the meanings of words, phrases, and sentences), and **orthography** (letters and letter patterns). We will consider these aspects in some depth in later modules, as well as **discourse pragmatics**—how we use language socially and contextually to communicate ideas. The context processor enables us to decipher a word's meaning from its sentence or topic context.

Each language processor gives information to the other processors (see *Figure 1.1*). This network of processors plays an essential role in language functions. All the parts of the reading brain must work together with fluency and synchrony. Before we go further in explaining how the processors interact, we must define some often-confused terms.

Terminology Counts! Defining the "Phon" Words

Before we go further in explaining how the processors interact, we must define some often-confused terms. What is the difference between the terms *phonological processing*, *phonetics*, *phoneme awareness*, and *phonics*? Only those who have some formal training in linguistics—such as speech/language pathologists, voice and diction teachers, or students of the world's languages—are likely to know! The terms refer to concepts and are not interchangeable. They all pertain to unique aspects of language processing that play a central role in learning to read, spell, and write.

The root *phon* in the words **phonological**, **phonetic**, **phonemic**, and **phonic** is derived from the Greek root for "vocal sound." The notes of a symphony, the clang of a garbage-can lid, and the roar of a sea lion are *auditory*, but not *linguistic*. Networks in the brain that process environmental sounds are distinct from networks that are responsible for language comprehension and production.

"You have the wrong number. No one whose name is
pronounced that way lives here."

Exercise 1.1 | Phonology Terms Graphic Organizer

- Complete this exercise as the phonology terms are defined and discussed in the phonology reading that follows.

- Fill in the major topics in boxes 1–4 and the subtopics as they are outlined in the text. Add your own "branches" or notes for each main topic.

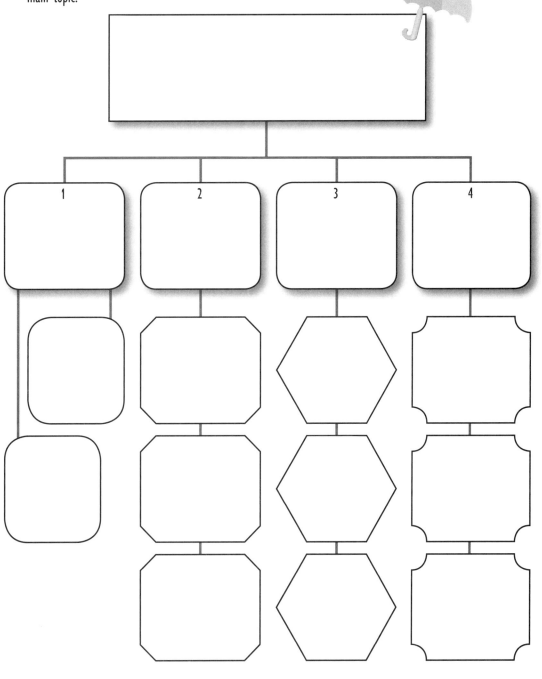

Phonology

Phonology is the science of vocal sounds and especially the study of the sound system within a language. The study of a phonological language system would include the order in which speech sounds (phonemes) are combined; the accent or stress patterns typically applied to words and phrases; and the ways in which speech sounds change if they are preceded or followed by other sounds. Terms that are included in the study of phonology are defined and explained with reference to the standard advocated by Scarborough and Brady (2002).

Phonological Processing

Phonological processing is an umbrella term used often in this module. Phonological processing refers to the mental formation, retention, and/or use of speech codes either in the performance of a cognitive or linguistic task or during language operations such as speaking, listening, remembering, learning, naming, thinking, reading, and writing. Phonological processes may be conscious or unconscious.

The **speech codes**, or **phonological representations**, that are used for language operations are mental images of the features of the sounds in words. Speech codes will be explained more as we discuss the features of phonemes. These mental codes may be out of focus, incomplete, or poorly established in students who have phonological processing problems (Brady, 1997).

Phonological processing is an aspect of many language tasks. It is impossible to measure it directly or to quantify how much any specific task may be dependent on phonological processing. Phonological processing encompasses three kinds of oral language skills—speech perception and production; phonological awareness; and phonological memory, retrieval, and naming—and also the processing of written language.

Speech Perception and Production

Speech perception and production are among the unconscious activities carried out by the phonological processor. **Speech perception**, also referred to as a *receptive language skill*, includes the abilities to distinguish between words that sound almost alike (e.g., **dusk/dust**; **fill/fail**) and to recognize any word that has been spoken. Speech is perceived by the brain as a set of acoustic signals or sound frequencies, formed by the vocal actions of a speaker.

Speech production is an *expressive language skill*. It includes the articulation or pronunciation of speech sounds and speech-sound sequences. Speech production errors involve the substitution of one sound for another (e.g., *wabbit* for **rabbit**; *dis* for **this**); the omission of a sound (e.g., *des* for **desk**); the addition of a sound (e.g., *artheritis* for **arthritis**); or distorting a sound (e.g., *echekate* for **educate**).

Teaching Tips

- Model proper pronunciation of Standard English.
- Ask students to repeat new vocabulary words, checking for proper pronunciation.
- Listen to students speak, providing positive corrective feedback when necessary.
- For students who receive speech services, communicate with the speech and language specialists about specific sounds to address; reinforce these sounds in your classroom.

Most people can use language effectively for communication purposes without being conscious of the sound, word, or phrase structures they are using. The next set of skills—phonological awareness skills—requires a higher level of thinking about the forms and functions of language, and is more closely related to reading and writing.

Phonological (Metalinguistic) Awareness

The term *metalinguistic* means above or beyond basic receptive or expressive language functions. The term *awareness* means conscious thinking about language itself. The focus of this module is **phonological awareness** (PA), the metalinguistic facility with the parts of words (Gillon, 2004).

Phonological awareness is the ability to identify, think about, and manipulate the parts of words, including syllables, onsets and rimes, and phonemes. It also includes the activities of recognizing and producing rhymes. Phonological awareness activities cultivate the ability to think about the internal details of the spoken word. The activities can be done using three units of language: syllable, onset and rime, and phoneme (see *Table 1.1*, next page). Awareness of words in sentences is more of a semantic, or meaning-based, skill than a phonological skill. We include a word awareness activity in *Table 1.1* because we can use whole words to begin teaching substitution, deletion, addition, or reordering of language parts.

Figure 1.2 (page 13) depicts the instructional progression by which speech-sound awareness (phonological awareness) becomes the foundation for learning orthography. This hourglass figure will be referred to many times in LETRS.

Table 1.1. Examples of Awareness Activities by Language Unit

Word Awareness	Sample Activity
A word has a consistent pronunciation and a consistent referent, or meaning, and has a place within sentence structure.	Orally say each word in a sentence while touching a chip or block that represents each word. | Our	cat	runs	fast.	

Unit of Language	Sample Activity
Syllable A unit of speech that is organized around a vowel sound. <div align="center">**dis-or-gan-i-za-tion**</div> <div align="center">**man-eu-ver**</div>	Tap your arm as you say each syllable. <div align="center">**cer-e-al**</div> <div align="center">**muf-fin**</div> <div align="center">**choc-o-late**</div>
Onset and Rime Two parts of any syllable. The *onset* is the sound(s) that come before the vowel; the *rime* is the vowel plus the consonant(s) that follow. **f—ish** **fr—esh** **squ—ish** **spl—ash**	Orally blend the two pieces of a syllable together. **cl + ean = clean** **h + am = ham** Note that *rhyming* involves the manipulation of *rimes*.
Phoneme The smallest segment of sound that differentiates words in a language system. **chose** = /ch/ /ō/ /z/ **those** = /th/ /ō/ /z/ (one sound change) **these** = /th/ /ē/ /z/ (one sound change) **threes** = /th/ /r/ /ē/ /z/ (two sound changes)	Say all the sounds in these syllables as you raise a finger for each sound. **each** = /ē/ /ch/ **know** = /n/ /ō/ **house** = /h/ /ou/ /s/

Figure 1.2. The Hourglass Concept, With Progression of Phonological Skills
(Contributed by Carol Tolman, used with permission.)

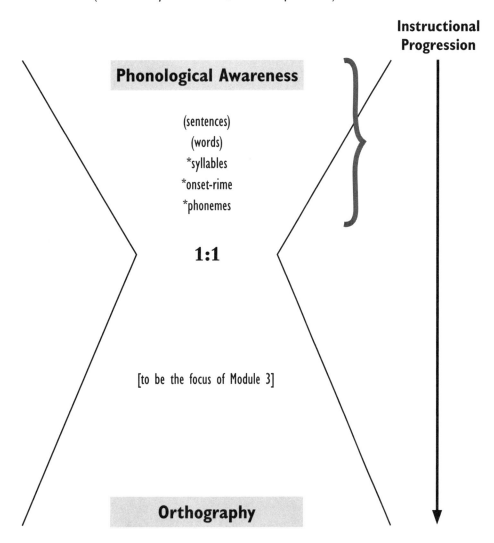

Instructional Progression

Phonological Awareness

(sentences)
(words)
*syllables
*onset-rime
*phonemes

1:1

[to be the focus of Module 3]

Orthography

★ Phonology steps most supported by research to improve reading and spelling skills

Teaching Tips

- Include phonological and phoneme awareness activities for students who need them—even older students and/or adults.
- Model or "think aloud" the mental activity of comparing confusable words.

Phoneme awareness and *phonemic awareness* are interchangeable terms. **Phoneme awareness** is demonstrated by any *oral language* task that requires attending to, thinking about, or intentionally manipulating the individual speech sounds in spoken words and syllables. Phoneme awareness is acquired gradually, usually after awareness of larger linguistic units (i.e., syllable, onset and rime). Phoneme and phonological activities can be done in the dark; they do not involve print. However, the processing of print in an alphabetic writing system requires phoneme awareness, and phoneme awareness is an important strand in the teaching of reading and spelling.

Phonological Memory, Retrieval, and Naming

Retaining phonological information in memory, retrieving phonological information from memory, and naming stimuli are also important phonological processes. These memory processes play a substantial role in reading and writing, and are often weak in students who experience difficulties with literacy acquisition.

Phonological memory, or **phonological working memory** (PWM), refers to temporary mental storage of speech stimuli. PWM is like a tape recorder with limited storage space. Stimuli are "taped over" constantly as we listen to and comprehend speech. We experience the limits of PWM when we: (a) try to remember a telephone number long enough to write it down; (b) recite a series of numbers backwards; (c) remember the directions to a destination; or (d) hold what we just read in mind while we read the next section of a book. Students who seem "spacey" or forgetful in these ways often have problems with PWM.

When we ask students to retell what they have heard, to follow a series of directions, or to repeat sentences before writing them down, we are taxing their phonological working memories. Only some of what we hear or read is extracted from PWM and sent to storage in **long-term memory** (LTM).

When speech information is stored in PWM or LTM, it is *encoded*. (The term *encode* also has another meaning: to spell by sound.) Tasks that measure the PWM span (i.e., the amount of speech information that can be held in a memory loop) include short-term and delayed recall of lists, such as lists of words, numbers, or speech sounds. Tasks that measure the quality of encoded information—that is, whether the person is storing accurate images of incoming speech signals—often involve repetition of words, including tongue twisters and nonsense words. These tasks are often structured to minimize the effect of word meaning.

Phonological retrieval, or retrieval of the phonological form of a word from LTM, refers to the mental act of formulating and pronouncing the word. When we cannot retrieve words that have been stored in memory, we may experience a "tip of the tongue" phenomenon or we may draw a blank even though we think we know what we want to say. Or, we may retrieve a word that resembles the word we want to say but which is inaccurate. Retrieval problems may originate with poorly specified or degraded phonological codes (representations) in memory, or with the retrieval process itself.

Recall that there are strong connections between the meaning processor and the phonological processor. When we speak, we draw words from our **lexicon**, or mental dictionary, pop them into sentence structures that will convey our intended meaning, and articulate the sounds so that a listener who speaks the same language can understand. The lexicon is the stored word bank in LTM. Words filed in the lexicon have sounds (phonological features) as well as units of meaning with assigned grammatical roles. We know the difference between **put** and **putt** because the words have different phonemes. Similarly, we know that **gas**, **glass**, and **grass** are separate words. Failure to retrieve words may be due to faulty storage of the word initially, or a faulty search-and-recall process. Retrieval problems affect us all and at times provide amusement, as with Lederer's (1987) catalogue of student bloopers, which includes this gem:

> J.S. Bach was a virtuoso who played many concerts and had many children. In between, he practiced in the attic on a spinster.

Imagine trying to remember a new word such as **dysdiodochokinesia**. When the sounds in a word are coded for long-term storage, the quality of the memory formed will depend on the attention given to those sounds, the accuracy with which the sounds were perceived, and the strategies employed to find a filing slot in memory from which that word can be retrieved. People who have trouble remembering words exactly as they first heard them are often affected by a more fundamental inability to form a complete, accurate image of all the sounds in the word. If a person thinks that **goal** is the same as **gold** or that **dyslexia** is **dylelia**, communication may be sabotaged.

> "My sisters gawked at the fascinating stranger and hung on his every syllabus of English . . ."
>
> —*The Poisonwood Bible* (Kingsolver, 1999, p. 128)

Teaching Tips

Give prompts and clues when students have memory, retrieval, and naming problems:

- Write down key words, cues, and phrases.
- Use visual prompts and graphic organizers.
- Pose a "choice" question ("Is it this or that?").
- Give the first sounds if you know the word the student is searching for.
- Ask students to repeat words orally.
- Review and summarize often.

Naming is a kind of retrieval. It involves producing the verbal label for a visually presented stimulus, such as an object or picture. **Rapid serial naming**, or **rapid automatized naming** (RAN), is a task in which repeated stimuli in an array, such as objects, colors, letters, or numbers, must be named as quickly as possible within a time limit. **Confrontation naming** is a term used for timed tests of labeling. There has been considerable theoretical debate about what these tasks measure (Goswami, 2000; Scarborough & Brady, 2002; Wolf & Bowers, 1999), but they do predict reading skill early in reading development.

Phonics and the Alphabetic Principle

The following terms pertain to aspects of reading and spelling that are dependent, in part, on phonological processes. Unlike the first three sets of terms, which are specific to oral language, these terms are relevant to the processing of written language. The **alphabetic principle** is the concept that English uses **graphemes** (letters and letter combinations) to represent phonemes. Grasping the alphabetic principle depends on phoneme awareness and familiarity with letters. Furthermore, syllable and morpheme patterns are represented in English spelling. *Figure 1.3* (next page) shows how phonology provides a foundation for learning print.

- **Phonics** is the system of correspondence between phonemes and graphemes, and also the approach to reading and spelling instruction that directly teaches students to use the correspondences to identify unknown words. The term *phonics* is sometimes used broadly to refer to any instruction in, or use of, print patterns that represent sounds, syllable patterns, and meaningful word parts (or morphemes). Beginning reading and spelling instruction that includes phonics has the edge over approaches that do not include phonics (Ehri, 2004; National Institute of Child Health and Human Development [NICHD], 2000).

- **Phonetic spelling**, or phonetically accurate spelling, describes spelling attempts that are unconventional or inaccurate. Phonetic spelling is that which faithfully represents the speech sounds in words, even though letters may be used in nonstandard ways (e.g., *klodz* is phonetically accurate for **clods**; *ejukate* is a phonetic spelling of **educate**). Good phonetic spelling is possible when a student has developed phoneme awareness. For this reason, tasks requiring phonetic spelling are sometimes used to assess phoneme awareness development.

Figure 1.3. The Hourglass Concept, Completed
(Contributed by Carol Tolman, used with permission.)

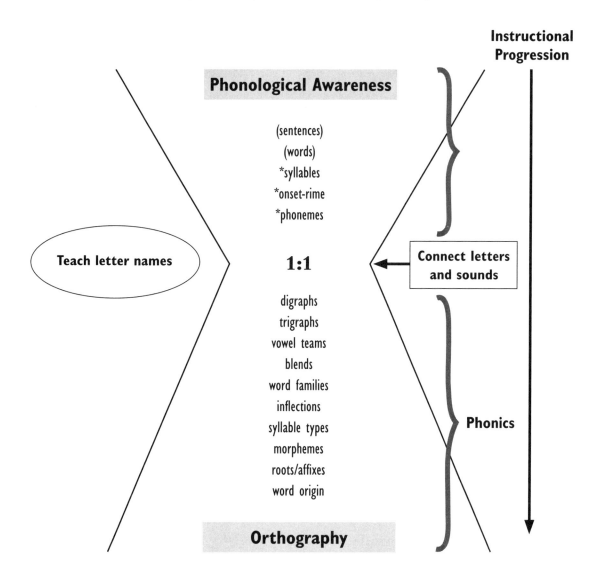

★ Phonology steps most supported by research to improve reading and spelling skills

Exercise 1.2 | Identify the Unit of Language

- The following items have been segmented. Listen to your instructor say each item.
- Identify whether the units of segmentation are words (W), syllables (S), onset-rimes (O-R), or phonemes (P). (Refer back to the examples in *Table 1.1* on page 12, if necessary. Some items may represent two levels of segmentation simultaneously.)

Item	Unit of Segmentation	Item	Unit of Segmentation
un-re-con-struct-ed		str-ing	
Good morning, America!		side-walk	
st-age		t-r-ee	
s-p-l-a-t		pl-ate	
fr-iend		po-ta-to	
happ-y birth-day		th-u-mb	
f-l-oa-t-s		sh-oe	

Why Phonological Awareness Is Important for Reading and Spelling

The phonological processor usually works unconsciously when we listen and speak. It is designed to extract the meaning of what is said, not to notice the speech sounds in the words. It is designed to do its job *automatically* in the service of efficient communication. But reading and spelling require a level of metalinguistic speech that is not natural or easily acquired.

On the other hand, phonological skill is not strongly related to intelligence. Some very intelligent people have limitations of linguistic awareness, especially at the phonological level. Take heart. If you find phonological tasks challenging, you are competent in many other ways!

This fact is well proven: Phonological awareness is critical for learning to read any alphabetic writing system (Ehri, 2004; Rath, 2001; Troia, 2004). Phonological awareness is even important for reading other kinds of writing systems, such as Chinese and Japanese. There are several well-established lines of argument for the importance of phonological skills to reading and spelling:

1. **Phoneme awareness is necessary for learning and using the alphabetic code.** English uses an alphabetic writing system in which the letters, singly and in combination, represent single speech sounds. People who can take apart words into sounds, recognize their identity, and put them together again have the foundation skill for using the alphabetic principle (Liberman, Shankweiler, & Liberman, 1989; Troia, 2004). Without phoneme awareness, students may be mystified by the print system and how it represents the spoken word.

   Students who lack phoneme awareness may not even know what is meant by the term *sound*. They can usually hear well and may even name the alphabet letters, but they have little or no idea what letters represent. If asked to give the first sound in the word **dog**, they are likely to say "Woof-woof!" Students must be able to identify /d/ in the words **dog**, **dish**, and **mad** and separate the phoneme from others before they can understand what the letter **d** represents in those words.

2. **Phoneme awareness predicts later outcomes in reading and spelling.** Phoneme awareness facilitates growth in printed word recognition. Even before a student learns to read, we can predict with a high level of accuracy whether that student will be a good reader or a poor reader by the end of third grade and beyond (Good, Simmons, and Kame'enui, 2001; Torgesen, 1998, 2004). Prediction is possible with simple tests that measure awareness of speech sounds in words, knowledge of letter names, knowledge of sound-symbol correspondence, and vocabulary.

3. **The majority of poor readers have relative difficulty with phoneme awareness and other phonological skills.** Research cited in Module 1 has repeatedly shown that poor readers as a group do relatively less well on phoneme awareness tasks than on other cognitive tasks. In addition, at least 80 percent of all poor readers are estimated to demonstrate a weakness in phonological awareness and/or phonological memory. Readers with phonological processing weaknesses also tend to be the poorest spellers (Cassar, Treiman, Moats, Pollo, & Kessler, 2005).

4. **Instruction in phoneme awareness is beneficial for novice readers and spellers.** Instruction in speech-sound awareness reduces and alleviates reading and spelling difficulties (Adams, Foorman, Lundberg, & Beeler, 1998; Gillon, 2004; NICHD, 2000; Rath, 2001). Teaching speech sounds explicitly and directly also accelerates learning of the alphabetic code. Therefore, classroom instruction for beginning readers should include phoneme awareness activities.

5. **Phonological awareness interacts with and facilitates the development of vocabulary and word consciousness.** This argument is made much less commonly than the first four points. Phonological awareness and memory are involved in these activities of word learning:
   • Attending to unfamiliar words and comparing them with known words
   • Repeating and pronouncing words correctly
   • Remembering (encoding) words accurately so that they can be retrieved and used
   • Differentiating words that sound similar so their meanings can be contrasted.

Sequence of Phonological Skill Development

Phonological skill develops in a predictable progression. This concept is important, as it provides the basis for sequencing teaching tasks from easy to more difficult. *Table 1.2* outlines the relative difficulty of phonological awareness tasks. *Table 1.3* (next page) is a more specific synthesis of several research reviews and summaries (Adams et al., 1998; Gillon, 2004; Goswami, 2000; Paulson, 2004; Rath, 2001) that ties specific ages to the typical accomplishment of those phonological awareness tasks.

Prerequisite to phonological awareness is basic listening skill; the acquisition of a several-thousand word vocabulary; the ability to imitate and produce basic sentence structures; and the use of language to express needs, react to others, comment on experience, and understand what others intend.

Table 1.2. Phonological Skills in Order From Most Basic to Advanced

Phonological Skill	Description
Word awareness	• Tracking the words in sentences. **Note**: This semantic language skill is much less directly predictive of reading than the skills that follow and less important to teach directly (Gillon, 2004). It is not so much a phonological skill as a semantic (meaning-based) language skill.
Responsiveness to rhyme and alliteration during Word Play	• Enjoying and reciting learned rhyming words or alliterative phrases in familiar storybooks or nursery rhymes.
Syllable awareness	• Counting, tapping, blending, or segmenting a word into syllables.
Onset and rime manipulation	• The ability to produce a rhyming word depends on understanding that rhyming words have the same rime. Recognizing a rhyme is much easier than producing a rhyme.
Phoneme awareness	• Identify and match the initial sounds in words, then the final and middle sounds (e.g., "Which picture begins with /m/?"; "Find another picture that ends in /r/"). • Segment and produce the initial sound, then the final and middle sounds (e.g., "What sound does **zoo** start with?"; "Say the last sound in **milk**"; "Say the vowel sound in **rope**"). • Blend sounds into words (e.g., "Listen: /f/ /ē/ /t/. Say it fast"). • Segment the phonemes in two- or three-sound words, moving to four- and five-sound words as the student becomes proficient (e.g., "The word is **eyes**. Stretch and say the sounds: /ī/ /z/"). • Manipulate phonemes by removing, adding, or substituting sounds (e.g., "Say **smoke** without the /m/").

Table 1.3. Ages at Which 80–90 Percent of Typical Students
Have Achieved a Phonological Skill

Age	Skill Domain	Sample Tasks
4	Rote imitation and enjoyment of rhyme and alliteration	**pool, drool, tool** "Seven silly snakes sang songs seriously."
5	Rhyme recognition, odd word out	"Which two words rhyme: **stair, steel, chair?**"
	Recognition of phonemic changes in words	"*Hickory Dickory Clock.* That's not right!"
	Clapping, counting syllables	**truck** (1 syllable) **airplane** (2 syllables) **boat** (1 syllable) **automobile** (4 syllables)
5½	Distinguishing and remembering separate phonemes in a series	Show sequences of single phonemes with colored blocks: /s/ /s/ /f/; /z/ /sh/ /z/.

	Blending onset and rime	"What word?"
		   th—umb
		   qu—een
		   h—ope

	Producing a rhyme	"Tell me a word that rhymes with **car**." (**star**)
	Matching initial sounds; isolating an initial sound	"Say the first sound in **ride** (/r/); **sock** (/s/); **love** (/l/)."

(continued)

Age	Skill Domain	Sample Tasks
6	Compound word deletion	"Say **cowboy**. Say it again, but don't say **cow**."
	Syllable deletion	"Say **parsnip**. Say it again, but don't say **par**."
	Blending of two and three phonemes	/z/ /ū/ (**zoo**) /sh/ /ŏ/ /p/ (**shop**) /h/ /ou/ /s/ (**house**)
	Phoneme segmentation of words that have simple syllables with two or three phonemes (no blends)	"Say the word as you move a chip for each sound." **sh—e** **m—a—n** **l—e—g**
6½	Phoneme segmentation of words that have up to three or four phonemes (include blends)	"Say the word slowly while you tap the sounds." **b—a—ck** **ch—ee—se** **c—l—ou—d**
	Phoneme substitution to build new words that have simple syllables (no blends)	"Change the /j/ in **cage** to /n/. Change the /ā/ in **cane** to /ō/."
7	Sound deletion (initial and final positions)	"Say **meat**. Say it again, without the /m/." "Say **safe**. Say it again, without the /f/."
8	Sound deletion (initial position, include blends)	"Say **prank**. Say it again, without the /p/."
9	Sound deletion (medial and final blend positions)	"Say **snail**. Say it again, without the /n/." "Say **fork**. Say it again, without the /k/."

Paulson (2004) confirmed the hierarchy of phonological skill acquisition (in *Table 1.3*) in 5-year-olds entering kindergarten. Only 7 percent of 5-year-olds who had not yet had kindergarten could segment phonemes in spoken words. The production of rhymes was more difficult for 5-year-olds than commonly assumed, as only 61 percent could give a rhyming word for a stimulus. Only 29 percent could blend single phonemes into whole words. Although some young students will pick up these skills with relative ease during the kindergarten year—especially if the curriculum includes explicit activities—other students must be taught these metalinguistic skills directly and systematically.

Keep in mind that student performance on phonological tasks can be accelerated through direct teaching and practice. The age at which students consolidate skills will depend, however, on their language exposure prior to school, home language context, familiarity with letter-sound correspondence, the school curriculum, and overall verbal proficiency.

Take 2 Review

- Revisit *Exercise 1.1* on page 9. Study the "phon" words in the graphic organizer you created, then re-create the organizer without referring back to it.

(continued)

- To a partner or small group, state five reasons why phonological awareness is important for learning to read and spell.

1. _____

   _____

2. _____

   _____

3. _____

   _____

4. _____

   _____

5. _____

   _____

Chapter 2 Discover the Speech Sounds of English

Learner Objectives for Chapter 2
- Pronounce the consonant and vowel phonemes accurately.
- Understand and be able to reproduce the consonant and vowel charts.

Warm-Up: Count Phonemes
- Try counting the speech sounds in each of these words. Hold up the number of fingers that correspond to the number of sounds you think are in each word.

  string ___   joyless ___   dodge ___   mixed ___   heard ___

  hippo ___   although ___   chew ___   house ___   few ___

Why Learn the Phonemes?

We expect that members of the group will disagree about the identity of phonemes in words, like those in the Warm-Up, until and unless we study what the phonemes are. On the surface, these are simple, common words that are likely to be taught in the primary grades; however, each represents certain complexities of speech. Disagreements about the identity and number of their sounds usually occur because:
- Phonemes are **coarticulated**, or smushed together in spoken words, and therefore are hard to separate.
- Adults pay attention to spelling more than to speech sounds, once they have learned to spell.
- Adults (especially teachers!) have learned different ways of classifying sounds.
- We have never studied the inventory of sounds.

Explicit knowledge of the phoneme inventory is not necessary to speak a language; it is only necessary for teaching a few subjects, including beginning reading and spelling.

What Is a Phoneme?

A **phoneme** is the smallest segment of speech in a language system that can determine word meaning, or that can be combined with other speech sounds to make a new word. For example, the words **cloud** and **clown** differ in one phoneme (the final consonant). The words **etymology** and **entomology** differ in one phoneme (**entomology** has one extra phoneme). The word **shoe** has two phonemes (/sh/, /ū/), the word **choose** has three phonemes(/ch/ /ū/ /z/), and the word **stove** has four phonemes (/s/ /t/ /ō/ /v/).

In English, we know that the speech sound /ā/ is a phoneme because it can be combined with either /b/ or /d/ to make the different words **bay** and **day**. The words **rich** and **ridge** also have different meanings and differ in one phoneme (the final consonant sound), so we can infer that /ch/ and /j/ are both phonemes in English. We use slashes (/ /) in LETRS to denote speech sounds and to distinguish them from letters. LETRS does not use the International Phonetic Alphabet (IPA), which can be found in Moats (2000). The IPA consists of individual symbols that represent all the phonemes, or speech sounds, in the English language.

English has about 44 phonemes. There are more phonemes than there are letters in English, and letters do not represent the phonemes simply or directly. To learn the phonemes, we must try to divorce our phonological processors from our orthographic processors. Forget (just temporarily) what you know about spelling.

Even professional linguists do not agree on how many phonemes there are or how they are classified—so no wonder educational materials are often confusing! Some languages (such as Hawaiian) have fewer phonemes than English, and some languages (such as Thai) have many more. Every language has a unique inventory of phonemes. For example, most of the speech sounds we call "short vowels" in English do not exist in Spanish, and Spanish has a front-placed, rolled /r/ sound, a voiced /th/ represented by the letter **d**, and a nasal sound /ny/, as in **piñon** and the adopted English word **canyon**. African languages sometimes include a "click" phoneme that does not exist in English. Many Asian languages distinguish vowel sounds by their vocal tone (similar to a high, medium, or low tone in singing) as well as their duration or length of pronunciation—features that English does not have.

Pronouncing a new language often involves learning to hear and form sounds that have never been wired into the brain's phonological processing system. Young learners have an advantage; their brains more readily assimilate new speech sounds. After about age 5, however, learning the phonology of a new language becomes more challenging as brain circuitry for speech production is already established.

Features of Articulation Distinguish Phonemes

Phonemes are distinguished from each other by the placement and action of the lips, teeth, and tongue during articulation, referred to as place and manner of articulation. **Place of articulation** has to do with whether the sound comes from the front, middle, or back of the mouth. **Manner of articulation** has to do with how the lips, teeth, and tongue are working to direct sound through the vocal tract (throat) and nose. We can describe a phoneme's *place and manner of articulation* by describing the **features**, or characteristics, of that phoneme. We can say that phonemes are contrasted and identified by their features. For example, a phoneme can be spoken **continuously** until we run out of breath, like the sound /ū/ or the sound /m/, or a phoneme can be a **stop**, like the sounds /k/ and /p/. Stop sounds must be pronounced with one short push of breath.

In addition, phonemes are distinguished by *voicing*. Some consonants are **voiced**, and all vowels are **voiced**; that is, they are spoken with the voice box turned on, or resonating. Some consonants are **voiceless** (or **unvoiced**)—spoken with the voice box turned off, like a whisper.

Another descriptive feature is *nasalization*. **Nasal sounds** drive the air through the nose. Most sounds in English drive the air through the throat and are non-nasal, or oral. Only three consonants in English are nasal: /m/, /n/, and /ng/.

As we present the consonants and vowels of English, we will describe them by their features or distinguishing characteristics, referring both to the place in the mouth where they are produced and the manner in which they are spoken.

Young Students Confuse Similar Sounds

Young students with underdeveloped phonological awareness often confuse the speech sounds that share features. That is, they confuse the sounds that sound or feel alike. They often speak and hear whole words without discovering the specific sounds that are in them. Thus, young students may not attend closely enough to hear the difference between **close** and **closed**, **shock** and **shark**, or **miss** and **mix**.

This is why LETRS teaches the *entire system* of phonemes, including their similarities and differences. An expert teacher knows which sounds are similar and confusable, and teaches students how to distinguish them. Teachers who can choose appropriate examples of sounds and words during instruction can head off confusion. Teachers should be able to say the sounds and model standard production. A student's internal representations of speech will be enhanced by informed instruction.

efry	for **every**	voiceless for voiced fricative
inems	for **items**	nasal for a stop
gat	for **grade**	omission of /r/ from blend; voiceless for a voiced stop
bag	for **back**	voiced for a voiceless stop
md	for **bed**	nasal for a stop

The Consonants of English

Phonemes can be divided into **vowels** and **consonants**. These terms describe phonemes as well as letters. In this module, a *consonant* refers to a phoneme. Consonants are produced with obstruction of the breath by the lips, teeth, and tongue. They are *closed sounds* because the breath is closed off in some way by the mouth. The English language has 25 consonant phonemes.

Consonant phonemes are described by their place and manner of articulation. The *place of articulation* refers to whether the sound is made in the front of the mouth, the back of the mouth, or in between the front and back. The *manner of articulation* refers to what the lips, teeth, tongue, vocal cords, and air stream are doing to form the sound. The table we will construct in *Exercise 2.1* shows place and manner of articulation of the consonants. Some consonants have vowel-like qualities, and not all consonants are equally accessible in spoken language. For both adults and children, some consonants are harder than others to perceive, pronounce, and unglue from the speech sounds around them.

Exercise 2.1 Explore the Consonant Phonemes of English

- Follow along as your instructor helps you explore the consonant phonemes. (It's best to use the Blank Consonant Phonemes Chart from the Handouts file because you will use it for later exercises.)

- Write each consonant phoneme inside slashes (/ /) in the appropriate box in *Table 2.1* as its place and manner of articulation is modeled and discussed. To avoid unnecessary complexity, use familiar letters (not the IPA) to represent the phonemes.[1]

Table 2.1. Blank Consonant Phonemes Chart

	Lips Together	Teeth on Lip	Tongue Between Teeth	Tongue on Ridge Behind Teeth	Tongue Pulled Back on Roof of Mouth	Back of Throat	Glottis
Stops Unvoiced Voiced	☐			☐		☐	
Nasals	☐			☐		☐	
Fricatives Unvoiced Voiced		☐	☐	☐	☐		
Affricates Unvoiced Voiced					☐		
Glides Unvoiced Voiced					☐	☐	☐
Liquids				☐	☐		

---

[1] Linguists use the International Phonetic Alphabet (IPA) to represent phonemes. We are avoiding this complexity, but advise anyone who is serious about learning phonology to become familiar with the IPA.

Stops

There are six **stops** in English; *stops* are made with one burst of sound. They contrast with **continuants**, such as the phoneme /s/, which can be held until the breath runs out. The six stops are in three pairs that contain one voiceless and one voiced phoneme. *Voiceless phonemes* are made with the vocal cords turned off. *Voiced phonemes* are made with the vocal cords engaged, or turned on. The presence or absence of voicing can be detected if you hold your hands over your ears. With the lips together, in the front of the mouth, we make two stop consonants: /p/ and /b/. Watch your mouth in a mirror and notice that the manner in which you speak these sounds is the same; they differ only in voicing. Hold your hands over your ears to hear the difference.

With the tongue behind the teeth, two other stops are made: /t/ (voiceless) and /d/ (voiced). Again, check in a mirror to see that the placement and manner of articulation of these phonemes is the same except for voicing. In the back of the throat, with the back of the tongue raised, are two more stops: /k/ (voiceless) and /g/ (voiced).

What kind of confusion is happening if a student writes *pasment* for **basement**? Or *sbidr* for **spider**?

Nasals

There are three **nasal** phonemes in English. The first, /m/, is made with the lips together. The second, /n/, is made with the tongue behind the teeth. The third, /ng/, is made with the tongue up against the back of the mouth. The phoneme /ng/ is the last sound in **song** and the next to last sound in **honk**. (The international phonetic symbol for /ng/ is /ŋ/.) *Nasals* are made by sending the air stream through the nose. Hold your nose and try to say these three sounds. (You can't!) Since the airflow goes through the nose and is different from other consonant sounds, young students often confuse these sounds in their reading and spelling.

Now, say the following consonants in sequence, noticing the similarity of place of articulation:

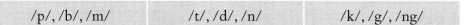

/p/, /b/, /m/	/t/, /d/, /n/	/k/, /g/, /ng/

Students quite commonly confuse these phonemes when they occur at the ends of words such as **sack**, **sag**, and **sang** or **back**, **bag**, and **bang**. Students who write *sig* for **sing** may be substituting one sound for another that is made in the same part of the mouth.

Fricatives

Fricatives are hissy sounds. A lot of friction is created when air is forced through small spaces in the mouth during articulation. There are eight *fricative* sounds in English: four unvoiced and four voiced. All eight are *continuants*; that is, we can say them until we run out of breath.

In the front of the mouth, /f/ and /v/ are made with the top teeth on the bottom lip; /f/ is unvoiced and /v/ is voiced. Check the similarity of these phonemes by looking in a mirror as you say them. Put your hand on your throat to feel the unvoiced /f/ and the voiced /v/ sounds and how they differ.

Moving back in the mouth, there are two consonants made with the tongue between the teeth. In English, these two consonants are spelled exactly the same way, so the reality of two "**th**" phonemes may be a surprise. One of the "**th**" phonemes is voiced and the other is unvoiced. The unvoiced /th/ begins the words **thick** and **thin** and ends the words **with** and **death**; the voiced /<u>th</u>/ begins the words **this** and **that** and ends the words **bathe** and **writhe**. This distinction is subtle, difficult for many people to hear, and not terribly important because the same digraph is used to spell both phonemes. The phoneme distinction contrasts some word pairs such as **ether** and **either**, **cloth** and **clothe**, **breath** and **breathe**, and **wreath** and **wreathe**.

The fricative pair /s/ and /z/ also differs only in voicing. The tongue is behind the teeth, and the sounds line up in the column under /t/, /d/, and /n/. These fricatives may be tricky to hear, especially when the letter **s** is used for the sound /z/, as in **hogs**, **wings**, and **rose**.

The final fricative pair is /sh/ (voiceless) and /zh/ (voiced). The phoneme /zh/ does not begin any words of English origin. It is found in words such as **genre** and **entourage** (French), **treasure** (French/Latin), and **azure** (Persian). Many phonics systems do not teach it at all because there is no unique spelling for this sound. Try this:

- Say /sh/ and /zh/. Say **garage** with /zh/.
- Say all the voiceless fricatives.
- Say all the voiced fricatives.

Affricates

Another two consonant sounds, /ch/ and /j/, combine features of stops with features of fricatives. They are made with the tongue pulled a little further back than it is for /s/ and /z/ and placed on the hard palate on the roof of the mouth. **Affricates** are different from *fricatives* because they stop air before releasing it. The voiceless /ch/ and voiced /j/ are formed similarly with the lips puckered. Words that show these contrasts are **cherry** and **Jerry**, **rich** and **ridge**. Try this:

- Say the sounds /ch/ and /j/.
- What kind of confusion is represented by the spellings *jili* for **chile** and *jokalet* for **chocolate**?

_____

_____

Glides

Glides, along with the liquids, have vowel-like qualities and readily combine with vowels. Glides are consonants that are always followed by a vowel phoneme and that literally glide right into that vowel. They include /w/ (voiced), /wh/ (voiceless), /y/ (voiced), and the glottal sound /h/ (voiceless). The consonants /y/ and /w/ are especially hard to separate from the vowel that follows them in phoneme awareness instruction. Young students have difficulty with glides in their reading and spelling. Try this:

• Say **yell** and **well**; say **help** and **whelp**; say **wile** and **while**; say **wither** and **whither**.

• Do you say the first sound of any of these words the same way? _____

_____

The voiceless glide /wh/, which is spelled **wh**, is losing its distinctiveness in American speech. Some linguists claim that it is completely lost at this point. Most Americans pronounce the beginning consonants in the words **whether** and **weather** the same way, although British speakers tend to retain the distinction between the voiced /w/ and the voiceless /wh/. For Americans, the distinction is a phonetic fiction promoted to help students remember which words have the **wh** spelling.

• Why do young students of English often confuse the spellings of **when** and **went**?

_____

_____

The glide /y/ is often placed in front of the vowel /ū/ (long **u**). In fact, the words **usual** and **unicorn** begin with consonant /y/, just like the words **you** and **Yule**. Words such as **cute** and **funeral** have the hidden glide /y/ before /ū/. This combination is often represented with the letter **u** in standard spelling. Try this:

• Say **ooze** and **use**. Which one begins with /y/? _____

• Circle the words that have /y/ + /ū/:

duke	educate	moon	immune	coup
cute	lampoon	puny	tune	fortune

The glottal sound /h/ is formed with the throat open and no other obstruction of air stream. It is always followed by a vowel. We say, "Harry ran home." We also say "a̲ historical event"—not "a̲n historical event"—because the /h/ is a consonant and the article **an** is used only before vowel sounds.

Liquids

The **liquids** /l/ and /r/ are slippery phonemes to describe, imitate, produce in isolation, or separate from vowels that precede them. *Liquids* are aptly named; they seem to float in the mouth. They influence vowels that come before them. Their pronunciation changes somewhat according to the sounds that surround them. /l/ is pronounced with the tip of the tongue lifted to touch the top of the mouth. /r/ is pronounced with both sides of the tongue touching the top of the mouth, and the tongue retracted. Because young students have difficulty feeling the presence of liquid sounds in words, these are two sounds that are often confused in student reading and spelling.

Some languages have no liquids at all. Others, notably Japanese and the Cantonese dialect of Chinese, have one liquid phoneme, pronounced like a combination of /l/ and /r/. Thus, English words with individual liquid sounds may be difficult for speakers of these Asian languages to articulate, and they may substitute /l/ for /r/. When liquids follow vowels, they change the vowels. Try this:

- Say **scored, scold, scour, scowl**.
- Describe what the liquids do to the vowels. _____

_____

_____

Syllabic Consonants

The liquids and nasals, including /l/, /r/, /m/, and /n/, can stand in for whole syllables when they occur at the ends of words of more than one syllable. In a word such as **button**, the last syllable is often pronounced like /n/. The vowel is there, but it overlaps with the consonant so much that we do not hear or pronounce a separate vowel segment. In the abstract, there is a vowel in every syllable, but when the vowel is blended (coarticulated) with a consonant in words such as **little** (/l/) and **better** (/r/), it becomes one sound standing for one syllable. Of course, /m/, /n/, /r/, and /l/ most of the time are nonsyllabic, single consonants—as in **need, mystery, red**, and **laugh**.

Young students' early spellings often omit vowel letters from final syllables pronounced like /l/, /r/, /m/, and /n/. The spellings are phonetically accurate because no separate vowel is articulated in these words. What words are these young students writing in the following examples?

ledr _____   *mitn* _____

lidl _____   *butn* _____

Try to say all of the sounds listed in *Figure 2.1* to a partner.

Figure 2.1. English Consonant Phonemes by Place and Manner of Articulation

	Lips Together	Teeth on Lip	Tongue Between Teeth	Tongue on Ridge Behind Teeth	Tongue Pulled Back on Roof of Mouth	Back of Throat	Glottis
Stops Unvoiced	/p/			/t/		/k/	
Voiced	/b/			/d/		/g/	
Nasals	/m/			/n/		/ng/	
Fricatives Unvoiced		/f/	/th/	/s/	/sh/		
Voiced		/v/	/th/	/z/	/zh/		
Affricates Unvoiced					/ch/		
Voiced					/j/		
Glides Unvoiced						/wh/	/h/
Voiced					/y/	/w/	
Liquids				/l/	/r/		

Students learn to articulate these sounds in a progression that is predictable according to the American Speech-Language-Hearing Association (Sander, 1972). This progression is represented in *Figure 2.2*, following.

Figure 2.2. Development of Consonant Articulation
(based on Sander, 1972)

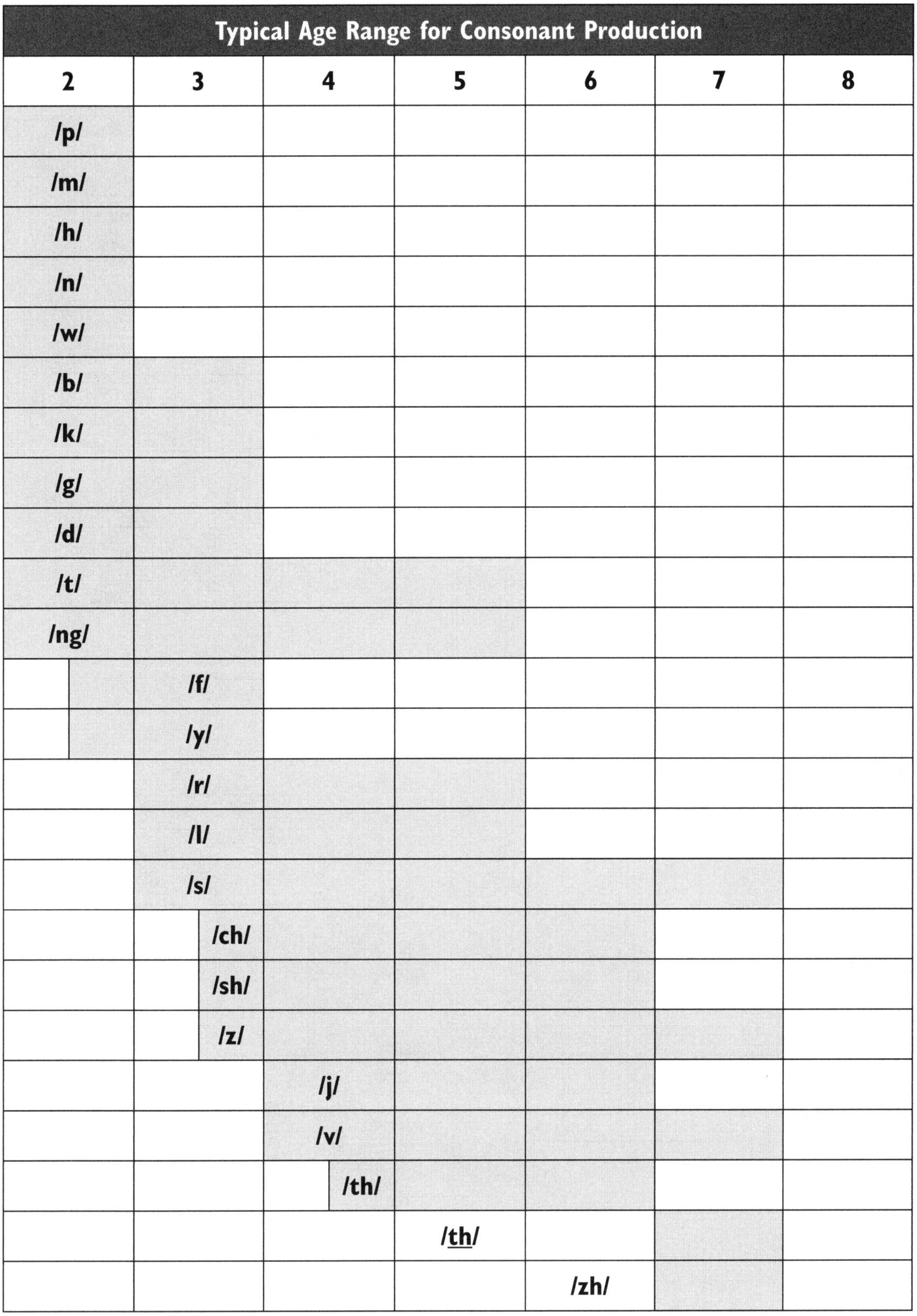

Typical Age Range for Consonant Production						
2	**3**	**4**	**5**	**6**	**7**	**8**
/p/						
/m/						
/h/						
/n/						
/w/						
/b/						
/k/						
/g/						
/d/						
/t/						
/ng/						
	/f/					
	/y/					
	/r/					
	/l/					
	/s/					
	/ch/					
	/sh/					
	/z/					
		/j/				
		/v/				
		/th/				
			/<u>th</u>/			
				/zh/		

Exercise 2.2 | Identify Beginning and Ending Consonant Sounds

- Identify, say, and write the symbol for the beginning and ending consonant sounds in each word. Don't be fooled by the word's spelling!

	Consonant Sounds				Consonant Sounds	
	Beginning	Ending			Beginning	Ending
come	_____	_____		bridge	_____	_____
seethe	_____	_____		knob	_____	_____
crave	_____	_____		young	_____	_____
cage	_____	_____		cache	_____	_____
rhyme	_____	_____		wrinkle	_____	_____
white	_____	_____		phone	_____	_____
one	_____	_____		united	_____	_____
gnat	_____	_____		thresh	_____	_____
hymn	_____	_____		psychic	_____	_____
queen	_____	_____		rouge	_____	_____
league	_____	_____		giant	_____	_____
whole	_____	_____		wage	_____	_____
rose	_____	_____		there	_____	_____
south	_____	_____				

Exercise 2.3 | Analyze Spelling Errors

- Consonant confusions may occur because consonants share features and students may not fully differentiate the phonemes in spoken words. A student's spelling can be a window into his or her understanding of the sounds of the language.
- Take a look at the following student misspellings. Try to identify the reason for these misspellings, using the organization of *Figure 2.1* (page 34) to explain why.

Target Word	Misspelling	Reason
fan	van	
sharp	charp	
brag	brak	
bed	md	
this	vis	
grade	grat	

Teaching Tips

- Analyze student spellings.
- Correct phonological errors by asking students to segment and identify the individual speech sounds they hear in the word.

The Characteristics of Vowel Phonemes

When asked to define a vowel, most teachers will say "**a**, **e**, **i**, **o**, **u**, and sometimes **y**." This answer refers to the number of vowel *letters*, not the number of vowel *phonemes*. **Vowels** are phonemes that are *voiced* and *open*. Vowels are produced with no obstruction of airflow through the mouth. Vowels are the heart of a spoken syllable; every syllable must have a vowel sound. English has about 15 vowel sounds plus the **r**-controlled, or vowel-**r**, combinations /er/, /ar/, and /or/. Vowels are essential; however, vowel sounds are quite variable from dialect to dialect and region to region.

Vowels carry the tune when we sing. It is possible to sing the words to any of your favorite songs by leaving off the consonants and singing the vowels. On the other hand, it would be impossible to sing with only the consonants.

English has many more vowel sounds than Spanish and other Romance languages. The spellings for those vowels are quite variable. It is vowels—in both their spoken and written forms—that give students of English reading and spelling the most trouble. The arrangement of vowels that appears in *Figure 2.3* may be used to begin a discussion of the vowel pronunciation differences among dialects of English and between English and other languages.

Figure 2.3. English Vowel Phonemes by Order of Articulation

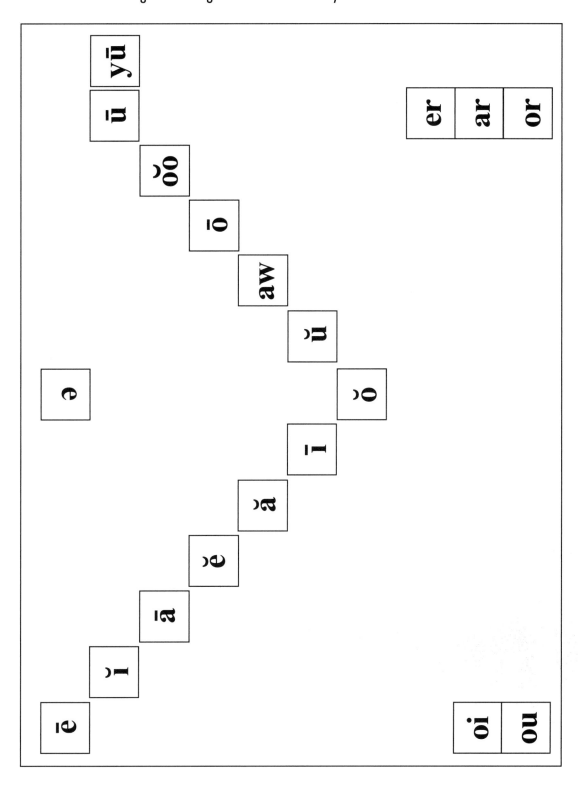

English Vowels by Order of Articulation

English vowels can be distinguished from one another by using the dimensions of tongue position (front, mid, back), tongue height (high to low), and lip shape (rounded and unrounded). The vowels can be contrasted by placing them between the consonants /b/ and /t/ (or a substitute when necessary) and forming a series of words (read down the columns):

beet	bot(tle)	boy
bit	but	bout
bate	bought	Bert
bet	boat	Bart
bat	put	(a)bort
bite	boot	

The vowel phonemes in *Figure 2.3* are arranged by position of articulation—front to back in the vocal cavity and high to low tongue position. The first vowel, /ē/, is formed with the lips in a smile position. It is a *high, front vowel* because the tongue is high up against the roof of the mouth and the sound is coming from the front of the mouth. As each successive vowel in the sequence is spoken, the tongue drops step by step and the mouth opens a little more until the wide-open *low, middle vowel* /ŏ/ is formed, as in the words **father** and **pot**.

Now, as you proceed to the next series of vowels, the mouth begins to close up. The tongue comes back up toward the roof of the mouth as the vowels in the back part of the sequence are spoken. The next vowel in the series, /ŭ/, as in **stuff** and **stubborn**, is sometimes perceived as being slightly in front of /ŏ/ and slightly higher in the mouth. It is a *low, middle vowel* similar to /ŏ/.

The next five vowels are *rounded, back vowels*. *Back* means that the tongue retracts toward the back of the mouth and the vocal resonance comes from farther back in the throat. As these four back vowels are spoken in order, the mouth closes slowly and the lips are held in a round shape: /aw/, /ō/, /ŏŏ/, /ū/, and /y/+/ū/. (Note that there are front rounded vowels in French [as in *tu* and *vieux*] and in German [as in *Tür* and *Müle*], but the only rounded vowels in English are these five back vowels.)

The **schwa** /ə/ floats in the middle of *Figure 2.3*. The word *schwa* means "empty" in Hebrew—an apt name for a deflated vowel whose stuffing has been removed. Schwa is an indistinct or neutral vowel sound that occurs only in unaccented syllables. Schwa is like /ŭ/ but is not accented. The low middle vowel /ŭ/ is identified in accented syllables (as in **but**, **butter**, **supper**). At times, schwa sounds more like /ĭ/, as in **def_inition** and **surf_ace**. Schwa is spelled many ways: **wag_on**, **_effect**, **reb_us**, **_aware**, **circ_uit**. One way to recognize a schwa is that it cannot easily be sounded out for spelling.

Two vowels that do not fit in the step-by-step sequence are the diphthongs /oi/ and /ou/. **Diphthongs** are single vowel phonemes that glide in the middle. The mouth position shifts during the production of the single vowel phoneme. When you say /oi/ slowly, notice how the mouth begins with a rounded /aw/ and then shifts or glides to a front, smiley position, /ē/. It shifts as well with /ou/ (as in "take a **bow** after a performance") from a front position (/ă/) to a lip-rounded position (/ū/).

The long vowel /ī/ is also considered by some to be a diphthong, but we place it next to /ŏ/ in *Figure 2.3* because young students tend to pair these sounds in spelling (e.g., writing *lot* for light).

Exercise 2.4 | Explore the Vowel Sounds of English

- Fill in *Table 2.2* (see next page) as your instructor reviews the sounds in order.

- Put your hand under your chin and look in a mirror as you say the sounds.

- Say the "front" vowels in order: /ē/ /ĭ/ /ā/ /ĕ/ /ă/ /ī/ /ŏ/. What is happening to your jaw, your mouth opening, and your tongue as you move down the sequence?

  _____

  _____

- Which are the "front" short vowels?

  _____

  Can you now explain why young students might confuse the vowels /ĭ/, /ĕ/, and /ă/?

  _____

  _____

  _____

- Say the "back" vowel sounds in order, holding your hand under your chin and looking in a mirror: /ŭ/, /aw/, /ō/, /o͝o/, /ū/.

  How is the mouth and tongue position changing as you say the sequence?

  _____

  _____

- When a vowel sound has two parts and slides in the middle, what is it called?

  _____

(continued)

Exercise 2.4 (continued)

Table 2.2. Blank Vowel Phonemes Chart

Are There Long Vowels and Short Vowels?

There are three categories of vowels—long, short, and diphthong (see *Table 2.3* below). Reading educators conventionally use the terms *long* and *short*, although they do not mean exactly what the terms imply. Long vowels are not always spoken for a longer time than short vowels. Say the words **bead** and **bid**. Then say **beet** and **bit**. The length of the vowel sound in those words is determined by the consonant that follows the vowel (/b/ is voiced; /t/ is unvoiced).

Linguists use different terminology to describe vowels. Long vowels are called *tense vowels*, and short vowels are called *lax vowels*. The terms *tense* and *lax* refer to the muscular tension in the jaw as the phonemes are spoken. The less common /ŏŏ/ and /aw/ vowels belong with lax (short) vowels with regard to the way they are spoken. However, since they are usually spelled with a vowel team, and their spellings are variable, they are not included in the set of short vowels taught in basic phonics.

Sometimes the long **i** is classified as a diphthong because it does slide or glide in the middle, as in **pie** (/p/ /ī/). The terms *long* and *short* are arbitrary; they have nothing to do with the length of time we say a vowel.

Table 2.3. Classification of Vowel Phonemes

Long (Tense)	Short (Lax)	Diphthong
beet	bit	(bite)
bait	bet	boil
boat	bat	bout
boot (/ū/)	pot	
beauty (/yū/)*	but	
(bite)	bought	
	book	

* Often long **u** is preceded by the glide /y/, as in **u̲se**, **c̲u̲te**, and **feu̲d**.

Vowel + r (Bossy "r")

When a vowel is followed by /r/, its sound usually changes. It may become totally combined with /r/, as in /er/, which is one indivisible phoneme. It may be slightly separated from /r/ but changed by /r/, as in /ar/ and /or/. Or it may keep its original sound, as in /ar/ (**fair**), /er/ (**fear**), and /r/ (**fire**). The spellings of these sounds are variable and difficult for young students to learn. As a result, many students with speech problems or phonological processing weaknesses may substitute phonemes for /r/ or have trouble pronouncing the sound. Blends with /r/ (e.g., **cr**, **sr**, **tr**) are also hard for them to spell.

Exercise 2.5	Match Words to Vowels on Your Vowel Phonemes Chart

- Work with a partner if you like. Identify the vowel sounds in the following words by writing the words underneath or next to the matching vowel sound on your blank Vowel Phonemes Chart on page 42. (Dialect may influence your choices.)

chew	heard	staff	vein	scythe	
hearth	chief	thou	calm	dove	scald
dread	choice	hymn	could	pour	most

- Which vowel is not represented?

  _____

- Compare notes with others. Which vowels are the most variable in regional dialects?

  _____

  _____

  _____

Exercise 2.6 Select Guide Words for Each Vowel Phoneme

- As you review each vowel phoneme in the sequence, think of a guide word, or key word, that you might use to teach young students about that vowel phoneme. Write it on your blank Vowel Phonemes Chart on page 42.

- To connect this next activity with your classroom, select a reading or spelling program that you use to teach students about the speech sounds of English. Then answer these questions:

1. Are there sound-spelling cards or posters in the program that teach the phonemes?

    _____

2. Did the program authors choose guide words that are good examples of the vowel phonemes?

    _____

3. Is the concept of a vowel sound taught explicitly? How?

    _____

    _____

    _____

    _____

4. Are all the vowels in English taught explicitly?

    _____

5. What is the teaching routine that helps students learn the vowel sounds?

    _____

    _____

    _____

    _____

Coarticulation

When we speak whole words, we combine phonemes in such a way that their features spread into one another. This is known as **coarticulation**, or literally "saying together." For example, say **desk** while looking at your mouth in a mirror. Then say **dress**. Notice that the /d/ in each word is formed differently in anticipation of the sound that will follow that phoneme. Our phonological processors direct our mouths to pronounce the sounds in words so that they will blend together easily.

Because of *coarticulation*, the separate identities of the phonemes may be obscured. This is especially true when consonants in the same column in *Figure 2.1* (page 34) exist in a cluster in a syllable. For example, in the middle of the mouth, the sounds /t/, /d/, /n/, /s/, and /z/ are all articulated with the tongue behind the teeth. In words such as **elephants** and **jumps**, the consonant clusters /nts/ and /mps/ at the ends of those words are spoken as coarticulated units. Students may have trouble differentiating or becoming aware of the individual phonemes in those consonant clusters. In such cases, seeing letters in written words actually helps students become aware of the sounds.

Take 2 Review

- Revisit the blank Consonant and Vowel Phonemes Charts (pages 29 and 42) you filled in. Learn all of the phonemes.
- Or, with a set of phoneme tiles written on self-stick notes, practice reconstructing the vowel and consonant phonemes charts from memory.

Chapter 3

Phonology and Spelling

Learner Objective for Chapter 3
- Recognize phonological influences on young students' spelling.

Warm-Up: Spelling Influences
- What might be influencing this young student's spellings?

> **Chuck liks to aet sum jilee ad sum jokolit.**
> *(Chuck likes to eat some chile and some chocolate.)*

Phonemes Are Elusive

Students must be able to identify the speech sounds in words before they can match symbols to those sounds in reading and spelling. If teaching students to be aware of phonemes in words were as simple as listing them and pronouncing them, however, instruction would be very straightforward. Unfortunately, phonemes are elusive; they change when they are put into words, and some are difficult to pronounce out of the context of a whole word.

Allophonic Variation

As explained earlier, phonemes in words are coarticulated, meaning they are spoken together as a seamless unit. There are no spaces between the phonemes in words such as /g/ /o͝o/ /d/ /m/ /or/ /n/ /ĭ/ /ng/. As a consequence, the features of phonemes spread from one to the other, like unfixed dye in fabric. In the process, phonemes are slightly changed. The results are called **allophones**—slight variations in pronunciation of a phoneme that occur automatically, such as the different /ĕ/ sounds in these words:

engine: The /ĕ/ is nasalized before /n/.

egg: The /ĕ/ sounds like /ā/ because the tongue pushes the vowel upward when it is followed by /g/.

edify: The /ĕ/ is closest to its "pure" form.

Phonemes are really categories of sounds that we perceive to be the same. Our listening brains generally ignore allophonic variation, or subtle differences in the way phonemes are spoken when they are put into words. Several kinds of allophonic variation, however, have readily observable effects on young students' spelling. Examining a few of these variations—aspiration, nasalization, flapping, and affrication—helps us understand how phonology mediates spelling development.

Aspiration

The voiceless stop consonants /k/, /p/, and /t/ are pronounced with a push of breath in the beginnings of syllables, before vowels, and if they are the first sound in a consonant blend. If /k/, /p/, or /t/ are the second sound in a blend, as in **skin**, **spun**, or **stem**, they are *unaspirated* or *deaspirated*: there is no push of breath. Young students are likely to mistake them for their voiced brothers (cognates) /g/, /b/, and /d/. Thus, young students may make these spelling substitutions:

sbydr (**spider**)	*sbesl* (**special**)
sdashn (**station**)	*sdrt* (**start**)
sgin (**skin**)	*sgary* (**scary**)

Final consonants /k/, /p/, and /t/ are also unaspirated or deaspirated and are more often confused with their voiced counterparts or omitted altogether in speech or spelling. This is one reason we teach initial consonants first: their features are more clearly articulated, so it is easier for young students to become aware of them.

Nasalization

Every vowel that occurs before a nasal consonant in English (e.g., /m/, /n/, or /ng/) becomes **nasalized**. That is, the vowel sound itself gets pushed through the nose, in anticipation of the nasal consonant that follows it. Say these word pairs while holding your nose:

bad, band
said, send
rat, rant
dote, don't
sick, sink
puck, punk

The reason that the final blends -**nt**, -**mp**, and -**nk** are hard for young students to spell is that the nasal sound gets lost in articulation. The nasal feature of the consonant bleeds into the vowel; the vowel anticipates and takes on the nasality of the consonant /m/, /n/, or

/ng/. The nasal consonant is articulated with a tongue gesture similar to the consonant that follows it, and it becomes part of one speech gesture. Sequences such as **-nt**, **-mp**, and **-nk** are coarticulated; thus, young students commonly misspell words such as:

sik (**sink**)	*juppy* (**jumpy**)
wet (**went**)	*siple* (**simple**)
basemet (**basement**)	

Students will have an easier time tuning in to the nasal sounds if they hold their noses during the pronunciation of words that have /m/, /n/, or /ng/ after a vowel.

Flapping

British speakers of English sometimes deride American English speech as lazy or sloppy. However, the "shortcomings" of American speech are committed by all Americans because the differences are rule-based; Americans speak the way they do because of dialect characteristics, not character lapses. One of the automatic, rule-based changes that American speakers make more than British speakers is to change /t/ to a tongue flap that sounds like /d/ when it is between an accented and unaccented vowel, such as in **water**, **better**, **writer**, **British**, and **little**.

Changing the middle /t/ to a tongue flap ("**flapping**") explains why young students make sensible spelling attempts such as *wadr*, *lidl*, *bedr*, *budr*, and *bridish*. The middle /d/ in words such as **rider**, **ladle**, and **skidding** is also reduced to a tongue flap. It is not pronounced the same way as the /d/ in **desk**.

Affrication

Teachers of kindergartners and first graders may have noticed the tendency of young students to spell this way:

chran (**train**)	*jrs* (**dress**)
chrick (**trick**)	*jragin* (**dragon**)
hret (**treat**)	*gran* (**drain**)
nachr (**nature**)	*ejukate* (**educate**)

When we pronounce /t/ or /d/ before /r/ or /y/, the /t/ and /d/ become **affricated**; that is, in anticipation of /r/, our mouths pucker up and the initial phonemes sound like /ch/ and /j/. Young students may use the letter **h** to spell /ch/ because **h** is the only letter name that has /ch/ in it. Likewise, they may use either **j** or **g** to spell the /j/ sound.

Spelling Is Influenced by Phonological Judgments

Early spelling development is shaped by a student's beliefs about the sounds in words. The realities of speech—including coarticulation of sounds and allophonic variation—cause some very common spelling mistakes or inventions until students know the right or conventional way to spell words. Phoneme awareness is necessary for learning the alphabetic principle and beginning spelling; on the other hand, identifying what the phonemes are is sometimes problematic. An informed instructor will recognize why young students use letters the way they do and will give corrective feedback about sounds, letters, and word structure when appropriate.

Exercise 3.1   Analyze Young Students' Writing

• Locate one or more words in each writing sample that show the phenomena listed under the sample.

> **Sample 1**: Sometime you can make pancakes with agg and with mike and you can make pancakes with buttr and grise.
>
> —End of second grade

— Use of a single letter for a syllable (/l/, /m/, or /r/):

_____ r in butter _____

— Omission or confusion of grammatical endings (e.g., **-ed**, **-s**, **-ing**):

_____ Sometime _____

— Substitution of one vowel for another vowel that is close in articulation:

_____ agg for egg _____

> **Sample 2**: I was also frighten when i was going home and i was by lots of trees and it was lighting. I was so frightened my that. Sometime thing could be so frightened that you could junp out of your shoes. Things that are frightingly can scare you that you will not no what happen to you. I hate frighened things.
>
> —End of fourth grade

— Omission or confusion of grammatical endings (e.g., **-ed**, **-s**, **-ing**):

_____ frighten —> frightened _____

— Substitution of one consonant for another pronounced similarly:

_____ junp —> jump _____

Exercise 3.1   (continued)

Sample 3: I went to the brthday. Me and Cassd made are bedroom into a hotid home. I shod my grem and grap.

—Beginning of first grade

— Omission of a nasal consonant after a vowel and before a consonant that is pronounced similarly:

hotid = haunted

— Use of letter names to stand for one or more phonemes:

_____

Sample 4: I am gini bee a devil for halawene. I am going tric treding for Halawene. I fed the sdrae [stray] cat uesterday.

—Beginning of first grade

— Flapping of a medial /t/, spelled with **d**:

treding —> treating

— Voiced/voiceless consonant substitution:

_____

— First sound spelled with a letter whose name has that sound:

_____

(continued)

Exercise 3.1 (continued)

> **Sample 5**: Then the witch came off her broomstc. Then the witch went ovr the gobrigh [drawbridge]. Than the witch noct on the door then the princess opind the door then the witch grab the princess and then the witct jragd that princess to her hows. Then a prince so the witch jragen the princss to her hows. Then the prince went aftr the witch bat the prince was to fat. Then the naxt dai the witch jragd the princss to a hi op towr with no stars no dor.
>
> —May of kindergarten[2]

— Affrication of /t/ or /d/ so that it is changed to /ch/ or /j/:

_____

— Use of a single letter for a syllabic consonant /l/, /m/, or /r/:

_____

— Substitution of vowels that are similar in articulation:

_____

> **Sample 6**: Apirl hand lenkin worked at the white house.
>
> —End of kindergarten (child lives in Washington, D.C.)

— Why is this good phonetic spelling for a kindergartener?

_____

_____

_____

Take 2 Review

- Gather some writing and spelling samples from young students you know or teach.
- Identify spellings that are: (a) phonetically inaccurate (i.e., do not represent the speech sounds in the word); (b) phonetically accurate (i.e., do represent the sequence of sounds in the word); and (c) examples of phonologically driven "errors" that can be attributed to the way we actually say sounds in words. Those would include: (a) affricated /t/ and /d/ before /r/ and /y/; (b) omission of a nasal sound after a vowel and before a consonant; (c) substitution of a voiced for a voiceless stop within a consonant blend; or (d) the use of the letter **d** for a tongue flap.

---

[2] This child had been taught through a very systematic phonetic system, *Focus on Phonemes*, by Jan Crosby and Pat Tyborowski. (For more information, go to the Web site: www.thephonicsformula.com.)

Chapter 4 Understanding Language Differences

Learner Objectives for Chapter 4
- Recognize that most dialect differences are rule-based.
- Compare the phonemes of Spanish to those of English.

Warm-Up: Speech Patterns
- Reflecting on your own speech patterns:
  - Can others identify where you were raised?
  - Do you have distinctive ways of pronouncing words that are the result of a regional dialect (e.g., East Coast, southern, midwestern, western)?
- Share briefly with a partner.

What Is Dialect?

A **dialect** is a version of a language. A *dialect* is spoken by a group of people who are separated socially or geographically from other groups. The speakers of different dialects understand each other because they share the same basic language system, but their speech varies systematically or predictably in phonology, word use, or grammar. *Dialect interference* in a school setting occurs if the phonology or usage of a student's dialect differs substantially from the dialect spoken by the teacher. Dialect interference can also occur if the student's dialect is substantially different from the Standard English forms in written text. Consider these differences between British English and American English terms for the same thing:

British English	American English
lift	elevator
petrol	gasoline
public school	private school
trousers	pants
pint	mug of beer

Ways of pronouncing words differ in various regions of the United States. In specific regions, words are confusable because they are pronounced the same way, as follows:

Boston	Washington	Tennessee	Texas	Southern California
farther = father (drop the /r/)	**wash** = warsh (insert /r/)	**oil** = all	**pen** = pin	**caught** = cot

Young students benefit from systematic comparisons between the more formal or Standard English used in print and their oral language, especially during writing instruction. The goal of such comparisons is not to change the way students speak, but to help them become conscious of words, to check spelling and writing, and to choose words according to what the situational context calls for. When we choose to speak or write a certain way that is appropriate for a specific social context, we engage in **code switching**. For example, we usually modify our speech to a more formal style when we are in the presence of authorities, but change to a nurturing style when we are in the presence of young students. Writing demands certain forms that speaking does not.

Only two of the most common dialects encountered in schools today—Spanish language-influenced English and African American Vernacular English—are outlined here. Those interested in pursuing this topic in more depth are referred to the work of Labov (1998).

Spanish Phonology

To help teachers anticipate phonological substitutions and confusions that Spanish-speaking English-language learners (ELLs) might present in the classroom, we can begin with a comparison of the Spanish and English phonological systems. If a speech sound of a second language is not in a speaker's first language, that phoneme may be difficult to identify, pronounce, and manipulate in phonological awareness exercises. This is especially true when children do not hear the English language in their environments before they are one year old. Spanish-speaking ELLs benefit from direct teaching of speech sounds in each language (August, Carlo, Calderon, & Proctor, 2005; Cardenas-Hagan, Carlson, & Pollard-Durodola, 2007; Leafstedt & Gerber, 2005). At this point, these students benefit from being taught both the sound and the *feel* of the sound in order to hardwire these missing English phonemes accurately into the phonological processor.

Spanish Vowels

In Spanish, there are fewer phonemes (21) than in English (40+). The greatest difference between these language systems is the number of vowels (five vs. eighteen, counting vowel-**r** combinations). The five Spanish vowels are easy to distinguish from one another, like the long vowels in English, and are represented with consistent spellings. In Spanish reading instruction, students are usually taught the vowel correspondences first. *Figure 4.1* shows the Spanish vowels.

Figure 4.1. Spanish Vowel Phonemes by Order of Articulation

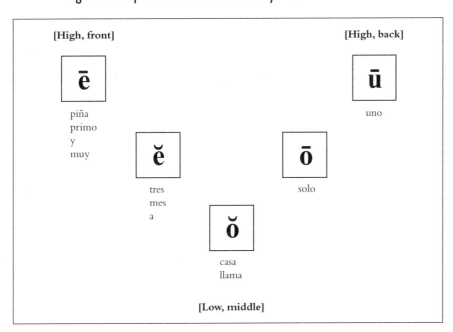

Two or three vowels often occur in sequence. Each retains its identity. In some words, two adjacent vowels belong to different syllables: **fiesta**, **Diablo**, **lea**. In some words, the adjacent vowels occur within the same syllable and are glided into one vowel sound: **cielo**, **muy**, **voy**, **puede**. *Trigraphs* are three vowels sequenced within one syllable, or one vowel phoneme with three parts: **buey**, **guia**.

| Exercise 4.1 | Compare Spanish and English Vowel Phonemes |

1. Circle the vowel phonemes in *Figure 4.2* (next page) that are not on the Spanish Vowel Phonemes Chart below.

2. Which English vowel sounds are likely to be most challenging for a Spanish-speaking learner of English to identify or to pronounce?

   _____

3. How could *Figure 4.2* help you explain the English vowel system to a learner of English?

   _____

   _____

   _____

Figure 4.1. Spanish Vowel Phonemes by Order of Articulation (repeated)

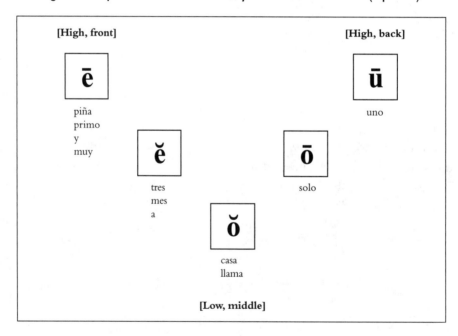

Figure 4.2. English Vowel Phonemes by Order of Articulation (repeated)

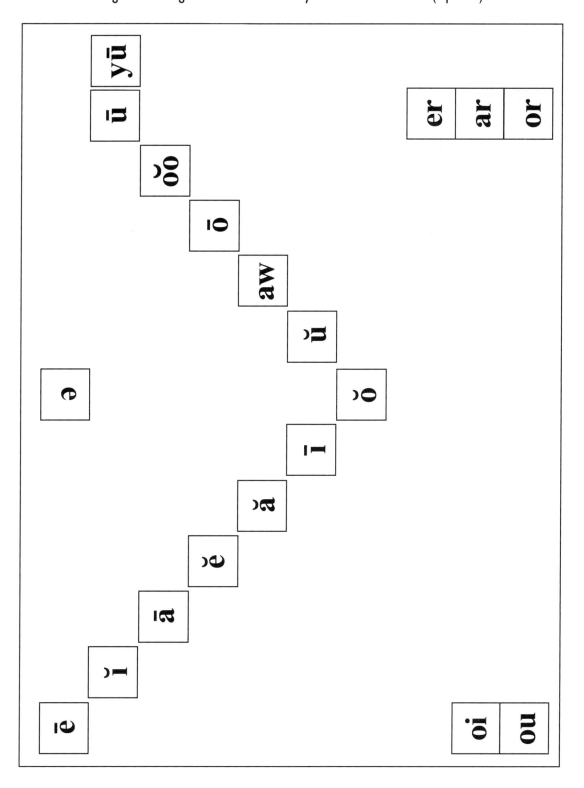

Spanish Consonants

With 16 consonants (see *Figure 4.3*) and 5 vowels, Spanish has 21 phonemes—only half the number of English phonemes. The 29 symbols used to represent those sounds have a much more consistent correspondence pattern than English. As with English speakers, Spanish-speaking students need practice identifying, segmenting, and blending phonemes; the patterns to be practiced, however, are usually open syllables that end with a vowel.

Figure 4.3. Spanish Consonant Phonemes by Place and Manner of Articulation

	Lips Together	Teeth on Lip	Tongue Between Teeth	Tongue on Ridge Behind Teeth	Tongue Pulled Back on Roof of Mouth	Back of Throat	Glottis
Stops Unvoiced	/p/ **pera**			/t/ **taza**		/k/ **que**	
Voiced	/b/ **bueno** **baca**					/g/ **gato**	
Nasals	/m/ **mano**			/n/ **nido**	/ñ/ **año**		
Fricatives Unvoiced		/f/ **fiesta**	/d/ **dos** (pronounced like voiced /<u>th</u>/)	/s/ **silla** **zapato**			/x/ **Mexico** (pronounced like hard /h/, as in the first sound in **jicama**)
Affricates Unvoiced					/ch/ **chile**		
Glides Unvoiced					/y/ **llama** **yo**		
Liquids				/l/ **limon**	/r/ **'rio** **barro**		

Figure 4.4. English Consonant Phonemes by Place and Manner of Articulation (repeated)

	Lips Together	Teeth on Lip	Tongue Between Teeth	Tongue on Ridge Behind Teeth	Tongue Pulled Back on Roof of Mouth	Back of Throat	Glottis
Stops							
Unvoiced	/p/			/t/		/k/	
Voiced	/b/			/d/		/g/	
Nasals	/m/			/n/		/ng/	
Fricatives							
Unvoiced		/f/	/th/	/s/	/sh/		
Voiced		/v/	/th/	/z/	/zh/		
Affricates							
Unvoiced					/ch/		
Voiced					/j/		
Glides							
Unvoiced						/wh/	/h/
Voiced					/y/	/w/	
Liquids				/l/	/r/		

| Exercise 4.2 | Compare Spanish and English Consonant Phonemes |

1. Look at the Spanish consonant phonemes in *Figure 4.3* on page 58.

2. Look at the English consonant phonemes in *Figure 4.4* on page 59.

   – Circle the English consonant phonemes that do not occur in Spanish phonology (i.e., those that are unique to English).

3. List the English consonant phonemes that a Spanish-speaking learner of English might need extra help in identifying or pronouncing:

Phonological Patterns of Spanish-Speaking Learners of English

To summarize, Spanish speakers who are learning English are likely to make rule-based changes to the pronunciation of English words, especially if they are first learning the second language at age 6 or above (when mastery of a new phonological system is usually more challenging than it is at age 5 or younger). The spellings of Spanish–speaking ELLs may reflect pronunciation patterns. These are the phonological changes most common for Spanish-speaking learners of English:

- /ch/ for /sh/
- /s/ for /z/
- /t/ or /d/ for /th/
- /ĕs/ for /s/ when /s/ is the first phoneme in a blend
  (The vowel pulls /s/ away from /k/, /t/, or /p/ in a blend, as in **Español**. Spanish-speaking students do not hear or pronounce **s**-blends before they learn English.)
- reduction of word-final consonant clusters

Spanish-speaking ELLs benefit from direct teaching of the sounds in each language, including how to pronounce the phonemes that are not familiar in Spanish. They also benefit from direct and systematic instruction of phoneme segmentation and blending.

Phonological Patterns of African American Vernacular English

Linguists and community members have debated whether African American Vernacular English (AAVE) is a dialect of Standard English or a language system deserving of its own name: Ebonics. No matter which perspective one embraces, AAVE has predictable and known phonological, syntactical, pragmatic, and semantic differences from Standard English (Labov, 1998). Many of these differences can be traced back to African languages spoken by the people who were enslaved and shipped to America in the 17th, 18th, and 19th centuries as well as the influence of the southern English dialect of slaveholders. Some common dialect features of AAVE are:

> **Teaching Tip**
>
> Use mirrors to help students practice sounds that are unfamiliar to them:
> - Model the sound and say, "Look in your mirror and make your mouth look like mine."
> - Have students feel their throats for voiced and unvoiced sounds.

- Reduction or simplification of consonant blends at the ends of words, when the blend includes two unvoiced or two voiced consonants:

toas'	*tes'*	*fac'*	*kep'*	*des'*
(toast)	**(test)**	**(fact)**	**(kept)**	**(desk)**

- Omission or confusion of inflections –**ed**, –**ing**, and –**s** (this is related to the consonant cluster reduction principle):

> *Sometime thing could be so frightened that you could jump out of your shoes.*

- Simplification of third-person singular verb (also, the word **agg** [below] represents both a vowel substitution and plural omission):

> *He like to make pancake with agg.*

- Initial /th/ pronounced /d/ (*dis* for **this**); medial /th/ pronounced /v/ (*brover* for **brother**); and final /th/ pronounced /f/ (*bof* for **both**). (African languages have no /th/ or /th/ sound.)
- Omission of the verb "to be," or using **be** to indicate an action of continuing duration:

> *He be waiting on you every single day!*

> *He waiting downstairs; hurry up!*

- Changing **ask** to *aks*. (Only this word is affected, as the consonant reversal does not occur in words such as **masking** or **skin**).

- Deleting or softening /l/ and /r/ after vowels. This is common to many southern American dialects, which in turn are related to southern British dialects:

> *Dat's a po' o'd dog.*
> (That's a poor old dog.)

There are many more differences among AAVE, Standard American English, and other regional and social dialects in the United States, but these few examples illustrate the predictable, rule-based characteristics that distinguish one form of speech from another. No dialect is inferior. A constructive teacher identifies, illustrates, and teaches important Standard English differences necessary for comprehending, speaking, reading, and writing using a neutral and factual approach.

Take 2 Review

- Identify typical ways in which the English language of Spanish-speaking learners of English and African American Vernacular English speakers differs from "standard" English.

	Spanish-speaking ELLs	**AAVE Speakers**
Phonology (production of speech sounds)		
Other		

Chapter 5 Teaching Phonological Skills

Learner Objective for Chapter 5
- Survey and role-play a variety of teaching activities.

Warm-Up: Your Resources for Teaching Phonological Skills
- What activities do you already use to teach phonological skills?
- What programs, program components, or supplements do you rely on?

For Whom Is Phonological Awareness (PA) Instruction Important?

Some kindergarten and first-grade students should start with the most basic listening, speaking, and word awareness skills and are not ready to start with manipulation of individual phonemes. These young students may be novices with insufficient preliteracy experience, or they may be dyslexic or language-delayed. They typically:
- score below benchmark on DIBELS® Letter Naming Fluency (LNF) and Initial Sound Fluency (ISF);
- do not "tune in to" or attend carefully to the sounds of language;
- are not aware that words can be broken into sound segments, such as onset and rime or syllables, and therefore are not ready for phonemic awareness instruction;
- cannot recognize or produce rhyme;
- may not know the terms *word, syllable, rhyme, letter,* or *first, second, third, last;*
- have limited experience with books and how they are read;
- may be ELLs or learners with limited English proficiency;
- may have experienced chronic ear infections, had ventilation tubes in their ears, or have difficulty hearing; and/or
- may have a parent or other relative who experiences difficulty learning to read and/ or spell.

Other students are ready to focus on phonemes. Students who benefit from direct teaching of phoneme awareness are those who are not yet able to segment and/or blend the single speech sounds in one-syllable words with accuracy and fluency. These students are recognizable because they:

- are typically below benchmark on DIBELS® Phoneme Segmentation Fluency (PSF);
- may not know the identity of all sounds in English (e.g., /sh/ and /ch/, or /w/ and /r/);
- may treat words as undifferentiated blobs of sound;
- try to guess at written words on the basis of one or two of the letters, instead of blending all the sounds together left to right;
- have trouble remembering how words are pronounced; and/or
- spell in ways that are not phonetically accurate (i.e., do not represent all the sounds in a word).

Older poor readers (above third grade) often need to build phonological skill as they learn to read and spell. About 90 percent of older poor readers show weaknesses in reading and/or spelling skills that depend on phoneme awareness. These weaknesses manifest themselves in a number of ways, including:

- the inability to sound out new words even though the student knows the letter sounds;
- limited automatic recognition of sight vocabulary, because of the problem with decoding;
- difficulty saying a word in syllables or saying the separate sounds in each syllable;
- poor spelling; and
- mispronunciation or confusion of similar sounding words, such as **Pacific** and **specific**.

Instruction that stimulates accurate and efficient phonological processing, no matter what the age of the student, will help students who demonstrate the common problems just described. That instruction may include planned, structured activities and continual, incidental linking of spoken and written language.

Teaching Phonological Skills: General Principles

1. Follow the order of phonological skills development (see *Table 1.2* in Chapter 1, page 20) and recognize the relative difficulty of each task. The goal of instruction is progressive differentiation of the *internal details* of the *spoken word* for deep, accurate representation in memory.
2. Focus students' attention on speech sounds before focusing on letters. Continue with phoneme awareness tasks until you are sure they can "tune in" to speech.
3. Encourage mouth awareness. Phonemes are speech gestures as well as speech sounds. Use mirrors. Ask students to determine whether their mouths are open or closed and whether they are using their tongue, teeth, or lips when they make the sound.

4. Include all English phonemes in the instruction. All phonemes can be taught, including all vowel sounds (such as /ŏŏ/ in **foot**) and sounds represented by digraphs (such as /ch/ in **itch** or /<u>th</u>/ in **that**).

5. Think *multisensory*. Involve students' hands, eyes, bodies, and mouths whenever possible.

6. A few brief activities—about 5–10 minutes per day—for 12–20 weeks are all that most students need to improve awareness of speech.

7. Show students what you want them to do [**I do**]. Practice together [**We do**], and then let students take turns while you supervise [**You do**].

8. Give immediate corrective feedback (e.g., if a student gives a letter *name* instead of a letter *sound*, explain the difference to the student and elicit the correct response).

9. Use letters to represent sounds as soon as young students are ready. Letters reinforce phoneme awareness and support it once students have learned to attend to sounds. *Figure 5.1*, the hourglass figure, illustrates the instructional progression from phonological awareness to decoding and spelling.

Figure 5.1. Instructional Progression From Phonology to Orthography
(Contributed by Carol Tolman, used with permission.)

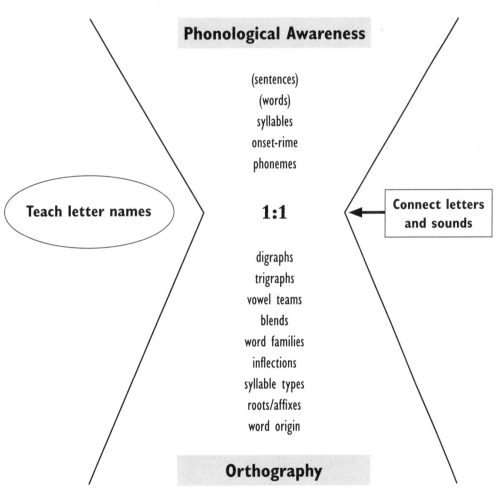

Phonological Awareness Activities for Preschool or Beginning Kindergarten Level

Break into small groups and prepare to demonstrate these activities for each other.

1. **Read Aloud**
   - Read books aloud with rhyme patterns and alliteration. Let students chime in and supply the rhyme or extend the alliteration.

2. **Rhyme Judgment**
   - Say: "Words rhyme if the last part of each word sounds the same. **Cake** and **bake** rhyme; so do **merry** and **cherry**. Listen while I say the poem, and get ready to say the rhyming word: *Jack and* **Jill** *went up the* **hill**. What words rhyme?"

3. **Rhyme Matching**
   - Say: "Listen carefully. Rhyming Robot wants to find a match for each of his favorite words. If one of his favorite words is **shake**, which of these words can he have: **meat**, <u>**steak**</u>, or **corn**?"

4. **Alliteration**
   - Say: "Peter Piper picked a peck of pickled peppers."
   - Say: "Let's make a silly sentence with /n/ words: *Neat Nancy . . .*"

5. **Syllable Blending**
   - Say: "Silly Caesar speaks very slowly. What word is Silly Caesar saying?"

ta-ble	hos-pi-tal	tan-ger-ine
roll-er-blades	fire-truck	play-ground

6. **Syllable Deletion**
   - Say: "Let's play a game with words. We're going to break some long words into parts and leave a part out. If I say **toothpaste**, and then leave off the **tooth**, what's left? That's right: **paste**. Let's try some more."

What's **baseball** without **ball**?	What's **butterfly** without **butter**?
What's **paddleboat** without **boat**?	What's **Sunday** without **day**?
What's **power** without **-er**?	What's **telephone** without **tele-**?

7. **Syllable Counting**
   - Say: "Inside this treasure chest are lots of things with names that you know. When it's your turn, reach in and take something out. Then tap the syllables as you say the word."

balloon	cricket	calculator	eraser
sharpener	stapler	candlestick	napkin

8. **Initial Sound Matching**
    - Say: "Let's see whose name starts with the same sound as someone else's name. They can stand together. **Tanya** and **Timmy**. What sound begins each of your names? Let's think of another name that starts with /t/."

9. **Onset–Rime Division**
    - Say: "Let's say some words in parts. I'll say the whole word. Then you say the whole word and divide it into two parts. Touch a colored felt square for each part, like this." (Model the technique first.)

c–ar	sh–ip	w–ave
p–ie	sk–at	d–esk

10. **Rhyme Production**
    - Say: "Let's play a game. I'll say three words that rhyme, and they sound alike at the end. You say one more word that rhymes. It can be a silly word. Let's start: **hinky, pinky, slinky,** _____."
    - Say: "Say a word that sounds like (rhymes with) **star**."

Exercise 5.1	**View a Video of Teaching Rhyme Production**

(*Teaching Reading Essentials* [Moats & Farrell, 2007], Part 1, Demonstration 4)

- Production of a rhyming word is difficult for many young students. This video demonstrates a technique for teaching the concept of rhyming. It begins by identifying the two parts of a syllable: onset and rime. The approach includes blending, segmenting, and making changes in those parts. The stage is then set for direct teaching of rhyme production.

- Materials for instruction include a magnetic white board and colored felt squares with magnets glued to the back.

- After viewing the demonstration, role-play the technique with a partner.

1. **Instructional Procedure: Blending a Word by Onset and Rime**
    - (**I do**) Say: "I'm going to say a syllable by two parts. Can you guess the word? Think, but don't say it. **s—ock**. Now, say it fast: **sock!**"

      [Alternative signal: Turn over one hand at a time as onset and rime are spoken, then bring hands together for the whole word.]

    - (**We do**) Guide group practice. Say each word slowly by onset and rime.

      Say: "Let's do some together. Listen and think: **ch—air**. Now, say it fast: **chair!**"

    - (**You do**) Call on individuals to say the parts, guess the word, and move their hands together as they say the word fast.

(continued)

Exercise 5.1 (continued)

2. **Instructional Procedure: Substituting Onsets to Create Rhyming Words**

   - (**I do**) Place two colored felt squares on the magnetic board for the onset and rime parts of a one-syllable word. Point to the corresponding square as you say each word part.

   Pass out a set of colored felt squares to each student.

   - (**We do**) Ask students to match the onset and rime sequence as you demonstrate. Touch and say the onset and rime parts of several more words as students copy your movements with their own squares. Point to either the onset or rime and ask, "What does this part say?"

   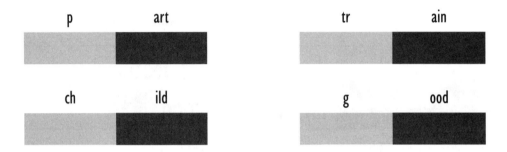

   - (**I do**) Say: "I'm going to change this part [point to the onset] to make a new word. The word is **child**." Change the color of the onset as you say the new sound(s). Say: "If I change /ch/ to /w/, I have **wild**. I changed **child** to **wild** by changing the first part and keeping the last part the same."

   - (**We do**) Continue giving guided practice, changing the onset to make a new word, and keeping the rime part the same.

   - (**You do**) After you have guided the practice, select a one-syllable word and ask students to think of a way the first part (onset) could change to make a new word with the last part. If they make a nonsense word, accept it but say that the word is a nonsense word—not a real word. Finally, say: "When the last part of words sound the same, the words are rhyming words."

Exercise 5.1   (continued)

More Difficult Phoneme Awareness Tasks

1. **Final Sound Matching**
   - Say: "Listen while I say two words. If they end with the same last sound, repeat the sound."

moon, pen /n/	bridge, page /j/	wish, mash /sh/	brick, steak /k/

2. **Blending Phonemes**
   - Say: "When I call your name, please stand. I'm going to say your name sound by sound."

/k/ /r/ /ĭ/ /s/	/h/ /y/ /ū/ /g/ /ō/	/w/ /ŏ/ /n/ /d/ /ə/

Exercise 5.2   Teaching Sound Blending

- Begin **blending** by combining syllables and compound parts into words. Progress to blending onsets and rimes and gradually move to sound-by-sound blending of two- and three-phoneme words. Consonant blends in words with four or more sounds are appropriate after simple syllables are mastered.

- The earliest oral blending exercises use words that begin with **continuous** consonants, not stops or affricates. Thus, /m/, /n/, /sh/, /th/, /f/, /v/, /s/, /z/, /sh/, /l/, and /r/ can be blended more easily than the stops /b/, /p/, /d/, /t/, /g/, /k/ or the affricates /j/ or /ch/. All the continuant consonants and vowels can be strung together to support blending (e.g., the sounds /v/ /ă/ /n/ can be held out to exaggerate their identity).

- Use the "touch and say" routine: Students say each sound as they point with their index fingers to the block representing the sound; then they blend the sounds together as they sweep their index finger from left to right under the blocks.

- Keyword picture cards, such as the sound-spelling cards from *Primary Spelling by Pattern* (Javernick & Moats, 2007), may be used for this activity, but with the letters covered up initially.

1. **Instructional Procedure for Blending**
   - (**I do**) Say: "I'm going to say some sounds slowly and you'll help me put them together to make a word. Listen." Put two colored squares on the board a few inches apart while you say: "/s/ /ē/." Push the colored squares together. Say: "Say it fast: **see!**"
   - (**We do**) Say: "Now you do it. Put out two colored squares that are not touching. Touch your colored squares while you say the sounds with me: /s/ /ē/. Now, push them together and say the word fast: **see!**"

(continued)

Exercise 5.2 (continued)

- Try a few more words with two sounds: /t/ /ō/—**toe**; /ā/ /k/—**ache**; /z/ /ū/—**zoo**. Say the sounds; then blend the word. Have students touch their squares and say the sounds while you model on the board. They can sweep a finger left to right while they "say the sounds fast."

- (**You do**) Students can practice as a group. Then, give each student a turn to repeat blending phonemes, using tiles to "touch and say" and blend the word.

(Module participants: Pair up and role-play this technique.)

Two-Phoneme Words	Three-Phoneme Words (No Consonant Clusters)	Four-Phoneme Words with Consonant Clusters
/g/ /ō/ (**go**)	/k/ /ē/ /p/ (**keep**)	/l/ /ă/ /m/ /p/ (**lamp**)
/ā/ /p/ (**ape**)	/g/ /ā/ /m/ (**game**)	/f/ /ĭ/ /s/ /t/ (**fist**)
/ē/ /ch/ (**each**)	/ch/ /ĭ/ /p/ (**chip**)	/m/ /ō/ /l/ /d/ (**mold**)
/ĭ/ /n/ (**in**)	/sh/ /ou/ /t/ (**shout**)	/g/ /r/ /ă/ /b/ (**grab**)
/ī/ /s/ (**ice**)	/b/ /ă/ /g/ (**bag**)	/k/ /l/ /ō/ /z/ (**close**)
/y/ /ū/ (**you**)	/k/ /oi/ /n/ (**coin**)	/s/ /t/ /ŏ/ /p/ (**stop**)
/sh/ /ī/ (**shy**)	/y/ /ĕ/ /l/ (**yell**)	/k/ /l/ /ou/ /n/ (**clown**)
/ar/ /t/ (**art**)	/s/ /ī/ /t/ (**sight**)	/f/ /l/ /ă/ /g/ (**flag**)
/ou/ /t/ (**out**)	/t/ /er/ /n/ (**turn**)	/w/ /aw/ /l/ /z/ (**walls**)
/b/ /oi/ (**boy**)	/r/ /ē/ /ch/ (**reach**)	/sh/ /ĕ/ /l/ /z/ (**shells**)

2. **Say It and Move It (Phoneme Segmentation)**
   - Say: "Listen to this word: **chick**. Say the word sound by sound while you move the counters in the boxes. Watch me first: (/ch/ /ĭ/ /k/). Let's do some together. Good. Which one is /k/? Which one is /ĭ/? What is the word?"
   - Say: "Now, it's your turn. Let's try some silly words (nonsense words)."

pem	zer	uff	zone	cheed

Exercise 5.3	View a Video of Teaching Phoneme Segmentation

(*Teaching Reading Essentials* [Moats & Farrell, 2007], Part 2, Demonstration 6)

- Blending is usually easier for young students than taking the sounds of a word apart. However, some students find segmentation easier than blending. Segmentation is much easier when students are already familiar with the individual speech sounds of their language and can associate a gesture or guide word with most of the sounds.

Instructional Procedure: Segmentation of Two-Phoneme and Three-Phoneme Words

- (**I do**) Point to the space with two sound boxes. Say: "I can break any word into its sounds. Listen. This one has two sounds: **at**—/ă/ /t/. Move two squares into the sound boxes while you say '/ă/ /t/.' What's the word? **at**."

- (**We do**) Say: "Let's do some together. We'll say the word, then move one block for each sound." Students repeat the word after you say it. Then, together with students, put a block into the two-square grid as they slowly say each sound.
  - Provide more practice with words with two sounds, demonstrating as students follow you: **toe**—/t/ /ō/, **toe**; **ache**—/ā/ /k/, **ache**; **zoo**—/z/ /ū/, **zoo**.

- (**You do**) Say a word, then ask students to repeat the word. Have students "say it and move it" with their blocks. Finally, have students sweep a finger left to right under the sounds while they "say the sounds fast." Give corrective feedback and model as necessary.

Alternate Technique: Finger-Stretching

- Explain to students that they will use their fingers to identify the sounds in words.
- Demonstrate the steps for students:
  1. Hold a fist in front of your body.
  2. Say a word with three sounds, such as **moon**.
  3. Beginning with the thumb, put up one digit as you say each sound in the word. For example, with the word **moon**, the thumb would represent /m/, the forefinger would represent /ū/, and the middle finger would represent /n/.
  4. Blend the sounds together as you close your fist, pulling it toward your body. For students who struggle with left-to-right orientation, move the arm across the body left to right when pulling together the sounds.

(continued)

Exercise 5.3 (continued)

Alternate Technique: Head, Waist, Toes

Use this technique with three-phoneme words:

- **(I do)** Say: "Watch me. I can take a three-sound word apart and touch one sound on my head, one sound on my waist, and one sound on my toes. I'll show you: **dish**."

  - Say /d/ as you touch your head with both hands, /ĭ/ as you touch either side of your waist with both hands, and /sh/ as you touch your toes (or knees).

  - Then stand straight, pull both fists toward your body, and say **dish**.

  - Ask: "Which sound is on my head? My waist? My toes?"

- **(We do)** "Let's do some together. The word is **reach**. Do and say with me." Repeat procedure in "I do" as students imitate you. Continue with other words: **can, soup, loud, pitch**.

- **(You do)** Each student gets a turn to repeat word and segment using head, waist, toes.

- Ask questions: "Where is [phoneme]? What is the 'waist' sound?" Continue asking questions.

Participant Practice, Segmenting Words Into Component Phonemes

- Use "sound boxes" and counters. Say the word first; then say each sound as you move a penny, chip, or block into a square. Finally, slide your finger under the whole word as you blend it back together. (Tell students how many sounds there are when you give them a word. The point of the task is oral production of separate phonemes, followed by blending them back together.)

- Words with four and five phonemes are complex syllables. They have consonant clusters or blends in them that are more challenging to segment than the simple syllables (without blends) in the first two sets.

Two sounds: **zoo, shoe, dough**

Four sounds: **post, jump, grab**

Three sounds: **mouse, cheese, song**

Five sounds: **stamp, shrink, plates**

Participant Practice, Initial and Final Sound Substitution

- Practice giving the following directions, using these examples or those of your own creation.

- Say: "Let's see if we can make some new words by changing just one sound. If I change /b/ in **bat** to /r/, what new word do I have? (**rat**) If I change /w/ in **wag** to /t/, what new word do I have? (**tag**) If I change /l/ in **shell** to /f/, what new word do I have? (**chef**)."

poodle–noodle	witch–win	race–rays

Exercise 5.3   (continued)

Middle Vowel Substitution

- Practice using colored blocks to explain vowel substitution.

- Say: "Now we'll make some new words by changing just one sound in the middle—the vowel sound. Here is **moose**: /m/ /ū/ /s/. Let's change **moose** to **mouse**. Which sound is changed? Only the middle one right here—the vowel sound."

moon–man	fawn–fin	soup–sap	boot–beet

Tracking Sound Changes with Colored Blocks (Sound Chaining)

- This technique is described in detail in *Exercise 5.4.*

Exercise 5.4   View a Video of Teaching Sound Chains

(*Teaching Reading Essentials* [Moats & Farrell, 2007], Part 2, Demonstration 7)

- Give students five blocks or chips with four different colors and one double. Different sounds are represented with different colored blocks, but blocks may represent any sound.

- Ask students to show the sounds in each dictated word using the blocks. You may add, change, delete, or switch the order of sounds in the dictated words, *one sound at a time* (e.g., if you change **day** to **date**, students would add a third block of a different color).

- Sometimes nonsense words or syllables are used in transitions from one word to the next. Try role-playing these sound chains with your instructor:

  1. **day, date, dot, pot, spot, spit, sit, sits**
  2. **me, mean, men, zen, zin, zip, chip, pitch, titch, stitch**
  3. **ouch, out, shout, shoot, shoes, use, dues, twos, stews**

Note: This is *not* a spelling activity. Since *sounds*—not letters—are being tracked, words that differ in only one speech sound do not have to be spelled the same way (e.g., words with digraphs and vowel-team spellings can be used because they represent one sound).

(continued)

Exercise 5.4   (continued)

1. **Instructional Procedure: Introduction to Sound Chains**

    *   (**I do**) Say: "Today we're going to listen for sounds that change in a word."

    *   Put three squares of different colors on the board as you say **night**. Say: "Touch and say: /n/ /ī/ /t/—**night**."

    *   Say: "I'm going to change something. This is **night**. Let's change it to **light**."

    *   Change the first colored square. Ask: "What did I change? That's right, I changed the first sound. I changed /n/ to /l/ to change **night** to **light**."

    *   (**We do**) Say: "Let's do some together. Listen for which sound changes. Show me **mess**. Now change **mess** to **guess**."

    *   Students say the word, put out three blocks, and then find which sound changed and change that color block. Students say which word they started with, what it changed to, and what sound changed.

        Note: If students know how to spell **mess**, they may want to use four blocks. Explain to them that they are using blocks to represent *sounds*, not letters. Only three blocks are needed.

    *   (**You do**) Give more practice, moving gradually to substitution of the last sound and then the middle sound. Words with three sounds that can be used include the following.

Beginning Change	Ending Change	Middle Change
knees—peas	dock—doll	tip—top
boat—note	room—rude	miss—mess
much—such	bath—bash	hope—hype

Exercise 5.4 (continued)

2. **Extension Activity: Longer Sound Chains**
    *   Students make changes to several words in a row. Sounds can be substituted, added, or deleted. Three more chains are illustrated below, in order of difficulty.

Three Sounds	One to Three Sounds	Blends
bit	rake	train
bet	ache	rain
bat	make	lane
sat	take	lame
sit	took	blame
mitt	book	claim
mat	hook	came
mad	hike	come
sad	hi	some
said	I	slum
bed	my	slump
bid	mine	lump

More Practice for Participants

*   Participants can practice longer and more varied sound patterns with the "Sound Chaining" activity in the Handouts Folder in the Module 2 Presenter's Kit.

Exercise 5.5 | Minimal Pairs (Advanced)

- A **minimal pair** of words differs only in one speech sound. Expert teachers can generate minimally contrasting pairs of words to provide appropriate practice hearing the contrasts between words. Practice distinguishing minimally contrasting pairs also helps ELLs hear sounds in English that may not be present in their first language.

- Look at the word pairs that follow. Think of another word pair that contrasts the same two sounds. See if you can think of words that contrast in the beginning sounds, ending sounds, and/or medial sounds. An example of each is given.

/ē/, /ĭ/ (**eat, it**; **bead, bid**)
seed   dip

/ā/, /ĕ/ (**fail, fell**)
whale   belt

/ĭ/, /ĕ/ (**pin, pen**)
skin   net

/ŭ/, /ŏ/ (**bud, bod**)
cut   hot

/ŏ/, /aw/ (**cot, caught**)
nod   crawl

/ou/, /oi/ (**plow, ploy**)
fowl   boy

/ch/, /j/ (**rich, ridge**)
church   edge

/f/, /v/ (**half, have**)
fat   wave

/l/, /r/ (**lock, rock**)
fall   car

/y/, /w/ (**yell, well**)
day   so

Sound Deletion

- Syllable: "Say **potato** without the **po**."
- Initial sound: "Say **peas** without the /p/."
- Final sound: "Say **sheet** without the /t/."
- Initial blend: "Say **stop** without the /s/."
- Final blend: "Say **wild** without the /d/."

Transition to Letter-Sound Correspondence

- Refer to *Exercise 5.2*, part 2 ("Say It and Move It") instructions to introduce a first set of six to eight grapheme tiles, such as **b, p, m, f, ee, v, t,** and **d**. (Note that **ee** and other two-letter combinations can be put on one movable tile because they are one sound-spelling unit. A grapheme represents a phoneme.)

- Teach the difference between "quiet" and "noisy" sounds that feel very much the same (i.e., /p/, /b/; /f/, /v/; /t/, /d/) as well as that /m/ goes through the nose.

Exercise 5.5   (continued)

- Use a guide word on a sound-spelling card to teach phoneme-grapheme associations. Reinforce associations through games and drills. Be sure that students can point to the right symbol for each sound as the sounds are dictated and then use the symbol to build simple words.

- Make a set of words with the grapheme tiles:

beet	deed	meet	peet	feet	feed	fee	vee	bee

- Possible order for adding other phoneme-grapheme associations:

1. /s/, /z/, /n/, /ă/

2. /k/, /g/, /ng/, /ŏ/

3. /sh/, /ch/, /j/, /ĭ/

4. /l/, /r/, /w/, /y/, /h/, /ŭ/

Note: Don't teach /zh/ or /wh/ until later.

Spelling Match Game

- Form two student teams. One student from Team A selects a word from a word bank or deck of word cards and reads the word aloud. [1 point for correct reading]

- Team B spells the word with tiles or written letters. If the team spells the word correctly [2 points], a Team B student takes the next turn as the word reader. If the word is not read or spelled correctly, Team B gets one more chance to fix the spelling [1 point if corrected].

Pig Latin

- Make a sentence by removing the first consonant from each word, putting the consonant at the end of the word, and adding the vowel **ay** to it. For example:

Hello, my name is Steve = Ello-hay, y-may, ame-nay, is-ay, teve-say.

Exercise 5.6 Examine Your Instructional Program

• Examine the Teacher's Edition of the reading, spelling, or literacy program you are teaching in your class. Identify the phonological awareness strand by looking at the comprehensive overview and unit overview pages. Then, answer the following questions.

1. Are the activities sequenced according to a developmental continuum? Where is that continuum explained?

_____

_____

2. Is phoneme awareness a consistent component of the daily lesson?

_____

_____

3. Does each activity focus on a linguistic unit (e.g., word, syllable, onset-rime, phoneme) that is appropriate for that level or that exercise?

_____

_____

4. Is oral language (phonemes) clearly distinguished from written symbol (letters) manipulation?

_____

_____

5. Is adequate practice provided?

_____

_____

6. Are the examples for the activities well chosen?

_____

_____

7. How will you measure progress with PA?

_____

_____

_____

Assessment of Phonological Skills

Learner Objective for Chapter 6

- Investigate tools for screening and diagnosing problems with PA.

Warm-Up: Assess Your Current Practices

- Does your school screen all students for reading problems?
- What evaluative instruments does your school use?
- How are the data analyzed and used to affect instructional choices?

Assessment for Evaluating Response to Intervention

Response to Intervention (RtI) approaches are now adopted by many districts to prevent serious reading problems and to reduce the number of students referred to special education. RtI models call for:

- screening all students;
- intensifying classroom reading instruction;
- using flexible groupings to provide extra instruction for students at risk; and
- giving concentrated direct instruction to students in the lower 10–20 percent of the distribution of skill.

All validated screening assessments that align with scientific research on the prevention of reading difficulties include a phonological assessment in kindergarten and first grade because phonological skills account for a significant proportion of variance in silent-passage reading comprehension at the end of third grade. Screening and diagnostic assessments often begin with phoneme segmentation and blending tasks because those tasks are the most reliable and accurate predictors—along with letter recognition—of word recognition and spelling. Students whose PA is underdeveloped will also have difficulty associating phonemes with graphemes during word reading and spelling tasks.

Direct assessment of PA is most purposeful and predictive of later reading and spelling with kindergarten and first grade students. It may also be informative with second grade and up, but assessments decline in validity and reliability as students get older (Hogan, Catts, &

Little, 2005). Why? Because the phonological component of word recognition is closely interwoven with word reading (real and nonsense words) and spelling as soon as students learn to recognize graphemes and words. Phoneme awareness is difficult to isolate, measure, and quantify reliably as a separate strand of the "reading rope" described in Module 1. In addition, tests of word reading and spelling—including oral reading fluency—are simply better predictors of overall reading skill after about second grade.

Nevertheless, we do encourage clinicians and reading teachers to use diagnostic assessments of phonological skills along with direct measures of reading, spelling, writing, and language no matter what the age of the student. Following are some suggested screening and prediction instruments and diagnostic inventories.

Screening and Prediction Instruments
- Dynamic Indicators of Basic Early Literacy Skills (DIBELS®) (www.sopriswest.com/dibels)
- Texas Primary Reading Inventory (TPRI) (www.tpri.org)
- AIMSweb® (www.aimsweb.com)
- Phonological Awareness Literacy Screening (PALS) (www.pals.virginia.edu)
- Children's Progress Literacy Assessment (CPLA) (www.sopriswest.com/cpi-literacy)
- IDEL™: Indicadores Dinámicos del Éxito en la Lectura (www.sopriswest.com/idel)
- Tejas Lee (www.tpri.org) (www.tejaslee.org)

Diagnostic Inventories
- Lindamood-Bell Auditory Conceptualization (LAC) Test—3rd Edition (www.proedinc.com) (www.linguisystems.com)
- Comprehensive Test of Phonological Processing (CTOPP) (www.sopriswest.com) (www.proedinc.com)
- Rapid Automatized Naming and Rapid Alternating Stimulus Tests (RAN/RAS) (www.proedinc.com)
- The Phonological Awareness Test (2007) (www.linguisystems.com)
- Really Great Reading assessments (www.rgrco.com)

Phonological Instruction for Older Students
Instruction that enhances awareness of speech sounds is relevant for older students who are inattentive to the internal details of spoken words. These students may show all the symptoms listed for younger students, including poor spelling, inaccurate decoding of new words, mispronunciation of words, and difficulty remembering or recalling new words. Direct teaching with a vowel chart and a consonant chart is quite possible with students at fourth grade and up, and many can improve substantially in PA with structured practice.

The phonological awareness strand of a well-designed reading or language lesson for older students includes brief, direct practice of specific skills such as syllabication or phoneme segmentation, often as a warm-up exercise before reading, spelling, or vocabulary instruction begins. In addition, these teaching activities and adjustments can be helpful:

- Ask students to recognize whether words have been pronounced correctly.
- Ask students to watch you as you pronounce new words or new names.
- Ask students to say vocabulary words aloud and to pronounce them correctly.
- Highlight, describe, segment, and pronounce individual speech sounds if similar sounding words are confused (e.g., **flush/flesh/fresh**; **entomologist/etymologist**; **gorilla/guerilla**).
- Use a guide word or gesture to remind students of a sound's identity, especially short vowels.
- Segment syllables and/or speech sounds before spelling words or to correct misspellings.
- Orally rehearse the repetition of phrases and sentences that are being written, to reduce the load on working memory.
- Write and talk when explanations are given; reduce the load on working memory.
- Provide written, pictorial, or graphic support when spoken language must be processed.

Summary

- *Phonological processing* is an umbrella term that encompasses many abilities having to do with speech perception and production; phoneme awareness; and memory, retrieval, and naming functions. In part, it accounts for how well an individual learns new words, pronounces words, learns a foreign language, recalls names and facts, and spells. *Phonological awareness* is a metalinguistic proficiency that includes the ability to divide a word into spoken syllables, onset-rime segments, and individual phonemes. *Phoneme awareness* is the component skill of phonological processing that is most closely related to reading and spelling. Learning to decode an alphabetic writing system with phonics requires phoneme awareness.

- Speech sounds are divided into consonants and vowels. Each speech sound is distinguished by a set of features, such as *oral* or *nasal*, *stopped* or *continuous*, *voiced* or *unvoiced*, and *aspirated* or *unaspirated* production. Speech sounds that are similar in place and manner of articulation are the most easily confused. If young students are left on their own to figure out the identity of speech sounds in words, they may not be able to detect all the features that distinguish those sounds. Speech sounds are not articulated separately; they are *coarticulated* when we speak, and thus, many people have some difficulty segmenting the sounds. Direct teaching is important because it enables students to form accurate concepts of speech sounds that will anchor their learning of vocabulary words and the writing system.

- Consonants are *closed sounds*. Consonants can be further categorized as *stops*, *nasals*, *fricatives*, *affricates*, *glides*, and *liquids*. There are nine pairs of *voiced* and *unvoiced* consonants that are otherwise articulated similarly.

- Vowels are *open sounds*. Vowels form the nucleus of every English word and syllable. They are classified on the dimensions of front, mid and back, and high to low. The front vowels are not rounded; the back vowels, however, are made with a rounding of the lips. Vowels may be *long* (tense), *short* (lax), or *diphthongs*. Vowels followed by /r/ have special properties.

- Identifying the existence of the speech-sound inventory is not an easy or obvious task because the sounds we think of as phonemes are buried in the continuous stream of speech that makes words, phrases, and sentences.

- English spelling is a less than optimal system for representing speech sounds. It has too few symbols (26) for the 25 consonants and 18 vowels, including vowel-**r** combinations. The six vowel letters are overworked in our writing system.

- Spanish has about half as many phonemes as English and only five vowels. Spanish is a more transparent writing system than English. The dialects of Spanish-speaking ELLs and AAVE speakers are characterized by regular phonological changes. Knowing these language differences helps teachers decide what contrasts among words to highlight when Standard English is being taught during language arts.

- Instruction in phonological awareness increases the likelihood that students will learn to read and spell with accuracy and fluency. Instruction in PA is essential for young students who show signs of early difficulty with sound identification. The PA component of reading and spelling instruction should be explicit, systematic, and informed by an understanding of the developmental progression of PA.

Final Quiz, Module 2

1. Complete the blank consonant and vowel phonemes charts given as handouts.
2. On a separate sheet of paper, list and explain four predictable ways in which student spelling attempts are likely to show the influence of speech-sound and word pronunciation.

    *   You may reference the phenomenon of *coarticulation* in the variations of how consonants and vowels are pronounced in words (allophonic variation) and reference the features of consonants and vowels.
    *   You may choose to reference your consonant and vowel chart handouts to show how sounds are confused.
    *   As a bonus, include misspelled words that illustrate spelling choices that students might make.
        Example: A student may spell all /ng/ sounds with **ng** (e.g., *chungk* for **chunk** or *singk* for **sink**). The sound represented by **n** in **chunk** and **sink** is /ng/ directly followed by the sound /k/, which, like /ng/, is articulated in the back of the throat.

3. Pick one of your examples above and briefly explain what kind of instruction or corrective feedback would help the student understand what phonemes really are in the word.
4. What are the phonemes in each of these words?

    show _____   knee _____   tax _____

    badge _____   enough _____

5. Explain the possible reasons why students made the following spelling errors:

Target Word	Spelling	Misspelled Word Explanation
sent	*sint*	
van	*fan*	
bed	*md*	
sink	*sik*	
real	*well*	

Glossary

Advanced concepts are indicated with an asterisk (★).

★**AAVE**: African American vernacular English, also called Ebonics or Black English; a dialect with phonological, semantic, and syntactic features that originated with African languages brought to the Americas by slaves

affix: a morpheme or a meaningful part of a word that is attached before or after a root to modify its meaning; a category that includes prefixes, suffixes, and infixes

★**affricate**: a speech sound with features of both a fricative and a stop; in English, /ch/ and /j/ are affricates

★**affrication**: the pronunciation of /t/ as /ch/ in words such as **nature**, and /d/ as /j/ in words such as **educate**

alphabetic principle: the principle that letters are used to represent individual phonemes in the spoken word; a critical insight for beginning reading and spelling

alphabetic writing system: a system of symbols that represent each consonant and vowel sound in a language

Anglo-Saxon: Old English, a Germanic language spoken in Britain before the invasion of the Norman French in 1066

base word: a free morpheme, usually of Anglo-Saxon origin, to which affixes can be added

★**bound morpheme**: a meaningful part of a word that makes words only in combination with other morphemes; includes inflections, roots, prefixes, and derivational suffixes

chunk: a group of letters, processed as a unit, that corresponds to a piece of a word, usually a consonant cluster, rime pattern, syllable, or morpheme

closed sound: a consonant sound made by using the tongue, teeth, or lips to obstruct the air as it is pushed through the vocal cavity

cognate: a word in one language that shares a common ancestor and common meanings with a word in another language

closed syllable: a written syllable containing a single vowel letter that ends in one or more consonants; the vowel sound is short

cluster: adjacent consonants that appear before or after a vowel; a consonant blend

★**coarticulation**:speaking phonemes together so that the feature of each spreads to neighboring phonemes and all the segments are joined into one linguistic unit (a syllable)

concept: an idea that links other facts, words, and ideas together into a coherent whole

consensus: agreement in the scientific community on specific truths that have emanated from a series of studies about a specific problem or issue

consonant: a phoneme (speech sound) that is not a vowel and that is formed by obstructing the flow of air with the teeth, lips, or tongue; also called a closed sound in some instructional programs; English has 25 consonant phonemes

consonant cluster (see *cluster*)

consonant digraph: a two-letter combination that represents one speech sound that is not represented by either letter alone

consonant-le syllable: a written syllable found at the ends of words such as **dawdle**, **single**, and **rubble**

context: the language that surrounds a given word or phrase (linguistic context), or the field of meaningful associations that surrounds a given word or phrase (experiential context)

context processor: the neural networks that bring background knowledge and discourse to bear as word meanings are processed

correlational studies: studies that show the strength of relationship between two or more variables, but that ordinarily are not sufficient to prove a causal relationship between or among those variables

cross-sectional: a type of study that draws samples of students from different age groups or grade-level groups

cumulative instruction: teaching that proceeds in additive steps, building on what was previously taught

decodable text: text in which a high proportion (i.e., 70–90 percent) of words comprise sound-symbol relationships that have already been taught; used to provide practice with specific decoding skills; a bridge between learning phonics and the application of phonics in independent reading of text

decoding: the ability to translate a word from print to speech, usually by employing knowledge of sound-symbol correspondences; also the act of deciphering a new word by sounding it out

★**deep alphabetic orthography**: a writing system that represents both phonemes and morphemes

★**derivational suffix**: a type of bound morpheme; a suffix—such as **-ity**, **-ive**, and **-ly**— that can change the part of speech of the root or base word to which it is added

dialects: mutually intelligible versions of the same language with systematic differences in phonology, word use, and/or grammatical rules

digraph: a two-letter combination (e.g., **th**, **ph**) that stands for a single phoneme in which neither letter represents its usual sound

diphthong: a vowel produced by the tongue shifting position during articulation; a vowel that has a glide; a vowel that feels as if it has two parts, especially the vowels spelled ou and oi; some linguistics texts also classify all tense (long) vowels as diphthongs

direct instruction: instruction in which the teacher defines and teaches a concept, guides students through its application, and arranges extended guided practice for students until mastery is achieved

discourse structure: organizational conventions in longer segments of oral or written language

double deficit: an impairment of both phonological processing and speed of word recognition

dyslexia: an impairment of reading accuracy and fluency attributable to an underlying phonological deficit

effect size: a statistic that measures the impact of an intervention on student performance in terms of standard deviation units

★**encoding**: producing written symbols for spoken language; also, spelling by sounding out

★**flap**: the tongue rising behind the teeth to produce a diminished /t/ or /d/ in the middle of words such as **water**, **better**, **little**, and **rudder**

★**fricative**: a consonant sound created by forcing air through a narrow opening in the vocal tract; includes /f/, /v/, /s/, /z/, /sh/, /zh/, and /th/

fluency: in reading, to read with sufficient speed to support understanding

generalization: a pattern in the spelling system that applies to a substantial family of words

★**glide**: a type of speech sound that glides immediately into a vowel; includes /h/, /w/, and /y/

grapheme: a letter or letter combination that spells a phoneme; can be one, two, three, or four letters in English (e.g., **e**, **ei**, **igh**, **eigh**)

inflection: a type of bound morpheme; a grammatical ending that does not change the part of speech of a word but that marks its tense, number, or degree in English (e.g., -**s**, -**ed**, -**ing**)

integrated: lesson components that are interwoven and flow smoothly together

★**lexicon**: the name for the mental dictionary in every person's linguistic processing system

*liquid: the speech sounds /l/ and /r/ that have vowel-like qualities and no easily definable point of articulation

logographic: a form of writing that represents the meaning of words and concepts with pictures or signs; contrasts with writing systems that represent speech sounds

longitudinal: a type of study that selects and then follows subjects over a long period of time

long-term memory: the memory system that stores information beyond 24 hours

*marker: in linguistics, a letter that has no sound of its own but that indicates the sound of another letter or letter combination, such as the letter **u** in the word **guard** that makes the /g/ a hard sound

meaning processor: the neural networks that attach meanings to words that have been heard or decoded

meta-analysis: a statistical analysis of the combined results of a series of studies that all address the same issue or problem

*metalinguistic awareness: an acquired level of awareness of language structure and function that allows us to reflect on and consciously manipulate the language we use

Middle English: the form of English spoken between the years 1200–1600, after the French Norman invasion of England and before the time of Shakespeare

*monosyllabic: having only one syllable

morpheme: the smallest meaningful unit of a language; it may be a word or part of a word; it may be one or more syllables (e.g., **un-inter-rupt-ible**)

morphology: the study of the meaningful units in a language and how they are combined in word formation

morphophonemic: having to do with both sound and meaning

multisyllabic: having more than one syllable

narrative: the type of text that tells about sequences of events, usually with the structure of a fiction or nonfiction story; often contrasted with expository text, which reports factual information and the relationships among ideas

NRP: Initialism for the Report of the National Reading Panel (National Institute of Child Health and Human Development, 2000)

onset-rime: the natural division of a syllable into two parts, the onset coming before the vowel and the rime including the vowel and what follows it (e.g., **pl-an**, **shr-ill**)

orthographic processor: the neural networks responsible for perceiving, storing, and retrieving letter sequences in words

orthography: a writing system for representing language

phoneme: a speech sound that combines with others in a language system to make words; English has 40 to 44 phonemes, according to various linguists

phoneme awareness (also, **phonemic awareness**): the conscious awareness that words are made up of segments of our own speech that are represented with letters in an alphabetic orthography

phonics: the study of the relationships between letters and the sounds they represent; also used as a descriptor for code-based instruction in reading (i.e., "the phonics approach" or "phonic reading")

phonological awareness: metalinguistic awareness of all levels of the speech sound system, including word boundaries, stress patterns, syllables, onset-rime units, and phonemes; a more encompassing term than *phoneme awareness*

phonological processor: a neural network in the frontal and temporal areas of the brain, usually the left cerebral hemisphere, that is specialized for speech-sound perception, memory, retrieval, and pronunciation

phonological working memory: the "online" memory system that remembers speech long enough to extract meaning from it, or that holds onto words during writing; a function of the phonological processor

phonology: the rule system within a language by which phonemes can be sequenced, combined, and pronounced to make words

★**pragmatics**: the system of rules and conventions for using language and related gestures in a social context

prefix: a morpheme that precedes a root and that contributes to or modifies the meaning of a word; a common linguistic unit in Latin-based words

qualitative research: research that relies on descriptive methodologies, including observational, case study, and ethnographic research; useful for hypothesis-generation

quantitative research: research that relies on measurement and statistical control of variables; preferable for determining cause and effect

randomized experiments: in research, experiments in which subjects are randomly assigned to the conditions that are being studied and compared

reading fluency: the speed of reading; the ability to read text with sufficient speed to support comprehension

root: a bound morpheme, usually of Latin origin, that cannot stand alone but that is used to form a family of words with related meanings

schwa: the "empty" vowel in an unaccented syllable, such as the last syllables of **circu̲s** and **bage̲l**

semantics: the study of word and phrase meanings and relationships

★**shallow alphabetic orthography**: a writing system that represents speech sounds with letters directly and consistently, using one letter for each sound

silent letter spelling: a spelling structure that consists of a consonant grapheme with a silent letter and a letter that corresponds to the vocalized sound (e.g., **kn, wr, gn**)

sound-symbol correspondence: same as *phoneme-grapheme correspondence*; the rules and patterns by which letters and letter combinations represent speech sounds

stop: a type of consonant that is spoken with one push of breath and not continued or carried out, including /p/, /b/, /t/, /d/, /k/, and /g/

structural analysis: the study of affixes, base words, and roots

suffix: a derivational morpheme (added to a root or base word) that often changes the word's part of speech and modifies its meaning

★**syllabic consonants**: /m/, /n/, /l/, and /r/ can do the job of a vowel and make an unaccented syllable at the ends of words such as **rhythm**, **mitten**, **little**, and **letter**

syllable: the unit of pronunciation that is organized around a vowel; it may or may not have consonants before or after the vowel

syntax: the system of rules governing permissible word order in sentences

vowel: one of a set of 15 vowel phonemes in English, not including vowel-**r** combinations; an open phoneme that is the nucleus of every syllable; classified by tongue position and height (e.g., high to low, front to back)

whole language: a philosophy of reading instruction that de-emphasizes the importance of phonics and phonology and that emphasizes the importance of learning to recognize words as wholes through encounters in meaningful contexts

word recognition: the instant recognition of a whole word in print

References

Adams, M., Foorman, B. R., Lundberg, I., & Beeler, T. (Spring/Summer, 1998). The elusive phoneme: Why phonemic awareness is so important and how to help children develop it. *American Educator, 22*(1 & 2), 18–29.

Arguelles, M., & Baker, S. (in press). *Teaching English language learners: A supplementary* LETRS® *module.* Longmont, CO: Sopris West Educational Services.

August, D., Carlo, M., Calderon, M., & Proctor, P. (2005). Development of literacy in Spanish-speaking English-language learners: Findings from a longitudinal study of elementary school children. *Perspectives: Quarterly Journal of the International Dyslexia Association, 31*(2), 17–19.

Brady, S. A. (1997). Ability to encode phonological representations: An underlying difficulty of poor readers. In B. Blachman (Ed.), *Foundations of reading acquisition and dyslexia.* Mahwah, NJ: Lawrence Erlbaum.

Cardenas-Hagan, E., Carlson, C. D., & Pollard-Durodola, S. D. (2007). The cross-linguistic transfer of early literacy skills: The role of initial L1 and L2 skills and language of instruction. *Language, Speech, and Hearing Services in the Schools, 38,* 249–259.

Cassar, M., Treiman, R., Moats, L., Pollo, T. C., & Kessler, B. (2005). How do the spellings of children with dyslexia compare with those of nondyslexic children? *Reading and Writing, 18,* 27–49.

Ehri, L. C. (2004). Teaching phonemic awareness and phonics: An explanation of the National Reading Panel meta-analysis. In P. McCardle & V. Chhabra (Eds.), *The voice of evidence in reading research* (pp. 153–186). Baltimore: Paul H. Brookes.

Gillon, G. (2004). *Phonological awareness: From research to practice.* New York: Guilford Press.

Glaser, D. (2005). *ParaReading: A training guide for tutors.* Longmont, CO: Sopris West Educational Services.

Glaser, D., & Moats, L. C. (2008). LETRS® *Foundations: An introduction to language and literacy.* Longmont, CO: Sopris West Educational Services.

Good, R. H., Simmons, D. C., & Kame'enui, E. J. (2001). The importance and decision-making utility of a continuum of fluency-based indicators of foundational reading skills for third-grade high-stakes outcomes. *Scientific Studies of Reading, 5,* 257–288.

Goswami, U. (2000). Phonological and lexical processes. In M. L. Kamil, P. B. Mosenthal, P. D. Pearson, & R. Barr (Eds.), *Handbook of reading research.* Mahwah, NJ: Lawrence Erlbaum.

Hart Paulson, L. (in press). *Early childhood* LETRS®. Longmont, CO: Sopris West Educational Services.

Hasbrouck, J., & Denton, C. (2005). *The reading coach: A how-to manual for success.* Longmont, CO: Sopris West Educational Services.

Hogan, T. P., Catts, H. W., & Little, T. D. (2005). The relationship between phonological awareness and reading: Implications for the assessment of phonological awareness. *Language, Speech, and Hearing Services in Schools, 36*, 285–293.

Javernick, E., & Moats, L.C. (2007). *Primary spelling by pattern: Level 1.* Longmont, CO: Sopris West Educational Services.

Kingsolver, B. (1999). *The poisonwood bible.* New York: HarperCollins.

Labov, W. (1998). Coexistent systems in African-American English. In S. Mufwene , J. Rickford, J. Baugh, & G. Bailey (Eds.), *The structure of African-American English* (pp. 110–153). London: Routledge.

Leafstedt, J., & Gerber, M. M. (2005). Crossover of phonological processing skills: A study of Spanish-speaking students in two instructional settings. *Remedial and Special Education, 26*, 226–235.

Lederer, R. (1987). *Anguished English.* Charleston, NC: Wyrick & Co.

Liberman, I. Y., Shankweiler, D., & Liberman, A. M. (1989). The alphabetic principle and learning to read. In D. Shankweiler & I.Y. Liberman (Eds.), *Phonology and reading disability: Solving the reading puzzle* (pp. 1–33). Ann Arbor: University of Michigan Press.

Moats, L. C. (2000). *Speech to print: Language essentials for teachers.* Baltimore: Paul H. Brookes.

Moats, L. C., & Farrell, L. (2007). *Teaching reading essentials.* Longmont, CO: Sopris West Educational Services.

National Institute of Child Health & Human Development (NICHD). (2000). Report of the National Reading Panel. *Teaching children to read: An evidence-based assessment of the scientific research literature on reading and its implications for reading instruction.* Washington, DC: National Institutes of Health. Retrieved December 5, 2007, from http://www.nationalreadingpanel.org/Publications/summary.htm

Paulson, L. (2004). *The development of phonological awareness: From syllables to phonemes.* ProQuest Digital Dissertations.

Rath, L. (2001). Phonemic awareness. In S. Brody (Ed.), *Teaching reading: Language, letters, and thought.* Milford, NH: LARC Publishing.

Sander, E. K. (1972). When are speech sounds learned? *Journal of Speech and Hearing Disorders, 37*, 55–63.

Scarborough, H. S., & Brady, S. A. (2002). Toward a common terminology for talking about speech and reading: A glossary of the "phon" words and some related terms. *Journal of Literacy Research, 34*, 299–334.

Torgesen, J. K. (1998). Catch them before they fall: Identification and assessment to prevent reading failure in young children. *American Educator, 22*(1 & 2), 32–39.

Torgesen, J. K. (2004). Avoiding the devastating downward spiral: The evidence that early intervention prevents reading failure. *American Educator, 28*(3), 6–9, 12–13, 17–19, 45–47.

Troia, G. (2004). Phonological processing and its influence on literacy learning. In C. A. Stone, E. R. Silliman, B. J. Ehren, & K. Apel (Eds.), *Handbook of language and literacy: Development and disorders* (pp. 271–301). New York: Guilford Press.

Wolf, M., & Bowers, P. G. (1999). The double-deficit hypothesis for the developmental dyslexias. *Journal of Educational Psychology, 91,* 415–438.

Instructional Materials for Teaching Phonological Skills

Adams, M., Foorman, B. F., Lundberg, I., & Beeler, T. (1997). *Phonemic awareness in young children: A classroom curriculum.* Baltimore: Paul H. Brookes.

Blachman, B., Ball, E. W., Black, R., & Tangel, D. (1999). *Road to the code: A phonological awareness program for young children.* Baltimore: Paul H. Brookes.

Dodson, J. (2008). *50 nifty activities for 5 components and 3 tiers of reading instruction.* Longmont, CO: Sopris West Educational Services.

Glaser, D., & Moats, L. C. (2008). *LETRS® Foundations: An introduction to language and literacy.* Longmont, CO: Sopris West Educational Services.

Grace, K. (2006). *Phonics and spelling through phoneme-grapheme mapping.* Longmont, CO: Sopris West Educational Services.

Greene, J. (2000). *Sounds and letters for reading and spelling.* Longmont, CO: Sopris West Educational Services.

Javernick, E., & Moats, L.C. (2007). *Primary spelling by pattern: Level 1.* Longmont, CO: Sopris West Educational Services.

Lindamood, P., & Lindamood, C. (n.d.). *The Lindamood phoneme sequencing program for reading, spelling, and speech* (LIPS). Austin, TX: Pro-Ed.

Nelson, R. J., Cooper, P., & Gonzalez, J. (2004). *Stepping stones to literacy.* Longmont, CO: Sopris West Educational Services.

O'Connor, R., Notari-Syverson, A., & Vadasy, P. F. (1998). *Ladders to literacy: A kindergarten activity book.* Baltimore: Paul H. Brookes.

Tyborowski, P., & Crosby, J. (2001). *Focus on /F/onemes: The complete phonemic awareness curriculum.* Worcester, MA: /F/onemes to Phonics.

Answer Key

Chapter 1
Phonology and Phonological Awareness

Warm-Up: Phonological Tasks (p. 5)

- Let your instructor lead you through these tasks. We expect that you may be unsure of some answers.

1. *Syllable Counting:* How many syllables are in each of the following words?

   theatrical __4__   appreciated __5__   fishes __2__

   cleaned __1__   scarcity __3__

2. *Rhyme Judgment:* Do each of these word pairs rhyme (yes or no)? Speakers may differ in their judgments.

   put, putt __No__   been, when __No__   loyal, toil __Yes__

   merry, scary __Yes__   on, yawn __Yes__   perk, Turk __Yes__

3. *Dialect:* Pronounce each of these words. Which pronunciations might reveal your regional or ethnic origins? **(All words)**

   ☑ tomato   ☑ parker   ☑ oil   ☑ caught   ☑ wash   ☑ sing

4. *Odd Word Out:* Which word does not begin with the same sound as the others?

   ❑ theory   ☑ therefore   ❑ thistle   ❑ thinker

5. *Phoneme Matching:* Which word has the same last sound as the word **does**?

   ❑ miss   ❑ nice   ☑ prize   ❑ purchase

6. *Initial Phoneme Isolation:* Isolate and say the first speech sound in each of these names.

   Eunice __/y/__   Charlotte __/sh/__   Wyatt __/w/__   Quinn __/k/__

(continued)

7. *Phoneme Blending:* Blend these sounds together to make a whole, real word.

    /th/ /ŭ/ /m/   __**thumb**__

    /m/ /or/ /f/ /ē/ /m/   __**morpheme**__

    /s/ /t/ /ă/ /k/ /s/   __**stacks**__

    /y/ /ū/ /n/ /ə/ /v/ /er/ /s/   __**universe**__

8. *Phoneme Segmentation:* Raise a finger for each sound as you break each of these words into its individual speech sounds (phonemes).

    shear /sh/ /ē/ /r/   **chains** /ch/ /ā/ /n/ /z/

    quite /k/ /w/ /ī/ /t/   **clutch** /k/ /l/ /ŭ/ /ch/

9. *Phoneme Deletion*
    - Say **driver**. Say it again without the /v/.   **drier**
    - Say **smoke**. Say it again without the /m/.   **soak**
    - Say **sink**. Say it again without the /ŋ/ (ng).   **sick**
    - Say **six**. Say it again without the /k/.   **sis**

10. *Phoneme Sequence Identification:* What is the <u>third</u> speech sound in each of these words?

    chunk __/ng/__   **bathe** __/th/__   **vision** __/zh/__   **exit** __/s/__

Exercise 1.1: Phonology Terms Graphic Organizer (p. 9)

• Complete this exercise as the phonology terms are defined and discussed in the phonology reading that follows.

• Fill in the major topics in boxes 1–4 and the subtopics as they are outlined in the text. Add your own "branches" or notes for each main topic.

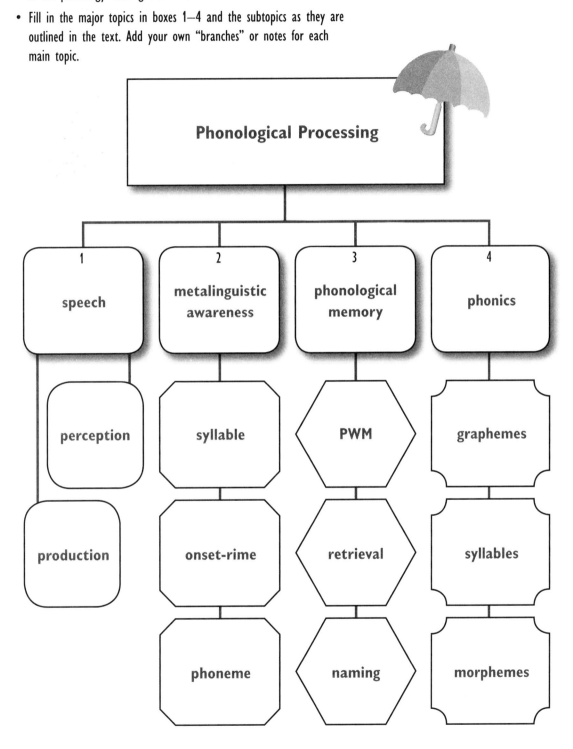

Exercise 1.2: Identify the Unit of Language (p. 18)

- The following items have been segmented. Listen to your instructor say each item.
- Identify whether the units of segmentation are words (W), syllables (S), onset-rimes (O-R), or phonemes (P). (Refer back to the examples in *Table 1.1* on page 12, if necessary. Some items may represent two levels of segmentation simultaneously.)

Item	Unit of Segmentation	Item	Unit of Segmentation
un-re-con-struct-ed	S	str-ing	OR
Good morning, America!	W	side-walk	W, S
st-age	OR	t-r-ee	P
s-p-l-a-t	P	pl-ate	OR
fr-iend	OR	po-ta-to	S
happ-y birth-day	S	th-u-mb	P
f-l-oa-t-s	P	sh-oe	P, OR

Take 2 Review (p. 24)

1. **PA is correlated with word decoding and spelling accuracy.**

2. **PA in kindergarten and beginning grade 1 predicts later reading achievement.**

3. **PA allows students to understand the alphabetic principle.**

4. **PA is often the core weakness in students with reading difficulties and/or dyslexia.**

5. **PA and vocabulary development are associated; if students have strong PA, they are more likely to learn the pronunciations and meanings of new words.**

Chapter 2
Discover the Speech Sounds of English

Exercise 2.1: Explore the Consonant Phonemes of English (p. 29)
(No Answer Key. Participants fill in Table 2.1 with instructor guidance.)

Affricates section (p. 31)
* Say the sounds /ch/ and /j/.
* What kind of confusion is represented by the spellings *jili* for **chile** and *jokalet* for **chocolate**?

  <u>Substitution of a voiced consonant for a voiceless consonant articulated</u>
  <u>similarly in all other respects. Substitution of a voiced affricate for a</u>
  <u>voiceless affricate.</u>

Glides section (p. 32)
* Say **yell** and **well**; say **help** and **whelp**; say **wile** and **while**; say **wither** and **whither**.
* Do you say the first sound of any of these words the same way? <u>**Most Americans**</u>
  <u>**say the last two word pairs with the same first sound: /w/.**</u>

The voiceless glide /wh/, which is spelled **wh**, is losing its distinctiveness in American speech. Some linguists claim that it is completely lost at this point. Most Americans pronounce the beginning consonants in the words **whether** and **weather** the same way, although British speakers tend to retain the distinction between the voiced /w/ and the voiceless /wh/. For Americans, the distinction is a phonetic fiction promoted to help students remember which words have the **wh** spelling.

* Why do young students of English often confuse the spellings of **when** and **went**?

  <u>**Because the "wh" spelling does not have a distinctive speech sound. The**</u>
  <u>**words sound alike. Also, final /t/ in "went" may not be articulated clearly.**</u>

The glide /y/ is often placed in front of the vowel /ū/ (long **u**). In fact, the words **usual** and **unicorn** begin with consonant /y/, just like the words **you** and **Yule**. Words such as **cute** and **funeral** have the hidden glide /y/ before /ū/. This combination is often represented with the letter **u** in standard spelling. Try this:

* Say **ooze** and **use**. Which one begins with /y/? <u>use</u>
* Circle the words that have /y/ + /ū/:

| duke | (educate) | moon | (immune) | coup |
| (cute) | lampoon | (puny) | tune | fortune |

Liquids section (p. 33)

- Say **scored**, **scold**, **scour**, **scowl**.
- Describe what the liquids do to the vowels. ___**The vowels are shaped by the**___ ___**mouth to blend with the /r/ or /l/. "Scour" and "scowl" sound as if they**___ ___**have an extra syllable.**___

Syllabic Consonants section (p. 33)

Young students' early spellings often omit vowel letters from final syllables pronounced like /l/, /r/, /m/, and /n/. The spellings are phonetically accurate because no separate vowel is articulated in these words. What words are these young students writing in the following examples?

ledr ___**letter**___   *mitn* ___**mitten**___

lidl ___**little**___   *butn* ___**button**___

Exercise 2.2: Identify Beginning and Ending Consonant Sounds (p. 36)

• Identify, say, and write the symbol for the beginning and ending consonant sounds in each word. Don't be fooled by the word's spelling!

	Consonant Sounds				Consonant Sounds	
	Beginning	Ending			Beginning	Ending
come	/k/	/m/		bridge	/b/	/j/
seethe	/s/	/th/		knob	/n/	/b/
crave	/k/	/v/		young	/y/	/ng/
cage	/k/	/j/		cache	/k/	/sh/
rhyme	/r/	/m/		wrinkle	/r/	/l/
white	/wh/ or /w/	/t/		phone	/f/	/n/
one	/w/	/n/		united	/y/	/d/
gnat	/n/	/t/		thresh	/th/	/sh/
hymn	/h/	/m/		psychic	/s/	/k/
queen	/k/	/n/		rouge	/r/	/zh/
league	/l/	/g/		giant	/j/	/t/
whole	/h/	/l/		wage	/w/	/j/
rose	/r/	/z/		there	/th/	/r/
south	/s/	/th/				

Exercise 2.3: Analyze Spelling Errors (p. 37)

- Consonant confusions may occur because consonants share features and students may not fully differentiate the phonemes in spoken words. A student's spelling can be a window into his or her understanding of the sounds of the language.
- Take a look at the following student misspellings. Try to identify the reason for these misspellings, using the organization of *Figure 2.1* (page 34) to explain why.

Target Word	Misspelling	Reason
fan	van	Voiced for voiceless consonant
sharp	charp	Fricative/affricate confusion
brag	brak	Voiceless for voiced consonant
bed	md	Both /b/ and /m/ are made with lips together
this	vis	/th/ and /v/ are voiced fricatives
grade	grat	/d/ and /t/ differ in voicing

Exercise 2.4: Explore the Vowel Sounds of English (p. 41)

- Fill in *Table 2.2* as your instructor reviews the sounds in order.
- Put your hand under your chin and look in a mirror as you say the sounds.
- Say the "front" vowels in order: /ē/ /ĭ/ /ā/ /ĕ/ /ă/ /ī/ /ŏ/. What is happening to your jaw, your mouth opening, and your tongue as you move down the sequence?

  The jaw slowly lowers as the mouth opens, and the tongue stays on the floor of the mouth.

- Which are the "front" short vowels?

  The "front" short vowels are /ĭ/, /ĕ/, /ă/.

  Can you now explain why young students might confuse the vowels /ĭ/, /ĕ/, and /ă/?

  The three "front" vowels are confused because they are articulated similarly; it is hard for children to differentiate them on the basis of how they are pronounced.

- Say the "back" vowel sounds in order, holding your hand under your chin and looking in a mirror: /ŭ/, /aw/, /ō/, /ŏo/, /ū/.

  How is the mouth and tongue position changing as you say the sequence?

  The mouth is slowly closing up and the lips are rounded. The tongue

  is pulled to the back of the mouth as the sequence is spoken.

- When a vowel sound has two parts and slides in the middle, what is it called?

  A diphthong.

Exercise 2.5: Match Words to Vowels on Your Vowel Phonemes Chart (p. 44)

- Work with a partner if you like. Identify the vowel sounds in the following words by writing the words underneath or next to the matching vowel sound on your blank Vowel Phonemes Chart on page 42. (Dialect may influence your choices.)

chew /ū/	heard /er/	staff /ă/	vein /ā/	scythe /ī/
hearth /ar/	chief /ē/	thou /ou/	calm /ŏ/	dove /ŭ/ scald /aw/
dread /ĕ/	choice /oi/	hymn /ĭ/	could /ŏo/	pour /or/ most /ō/

- Which vowel is not represented?

  /ə/ (schwa)

- Compare notes with others. Which vowels are the most variable in regional dialects?

  /ĭ/, /ar/, and /aw/ are often indicative of regional or cultural dialects,

  but many other vowels are characteristically changed in different

  regions of the country.

Exercise 2.6: Select Guide Words for Each Vowel Phoneme (p. 45)

  (No Answer Key. Responses will vary, depending on participant answers.)

Chapter 3
Phonology and Spelling

Exercise 3.1: Analyze Young Students' Writing (p. 50)

- Locate one or more words in each writing sample that show the phenomena listed under the sample.

> **Sample 1**: Sometime you can make pancakes with agg and with mike and you can make pancakes with buttr and grise.
>
> —End of second grade

— Use of a single letter for a syllable (/l/, /m/, or /r/):

buttr

— Omission or confusion of grammatical endings (e.g., -**ed**, -**s**, -**ing**):

Sometime

— Substitution of one vowel for another vowel that is close in articulation:

agg

> **Sample 2**: I was also frighten when i was going home and i was by lots of trees and it was lighting. I was so frightened my that. Sometime thing could be so frightened that you could junp out of your shoes. Things that are frightingly can scare you that you will not no what happen to you. I hate frighened things.
>
> —End of fourth grade

— Omission or confusion of grammatical endings (e.g., -**ed**, -**s**, -**ing**):

frighten, sometime, frightened, happen

— Substitution of one consonant for another pronounced similarly:

my / by; *junp* / jump

> **Sample 3**: I went to the brthday. Me and Cassd made are bedroom into a hotid home. I shod my grem and grap.
>
> —Beginning of first grade

— Omission of a nasal consonant after a vowel and before a consonant that is pronounced similarly:

hotid / haunted; *grap* / gramp

— Use of letter names to stand for one or more phonemes:

Cassd / Cassidy; *shod* / showed

Sample 4: I am gini bee a devil for halawene. I am going tric treding for Halawene. I fed the sdrae [stray] cat uesterday.

—Beginning of first grade

—   Flapping of a medial /t/, spelled with **d**:

treding / **treating**

—   Voiced/voiceless consonant substitution:

sdrae / **stray**

—   First sound spelled with a letter whose name has that sound:

uesterday / **yesterday**

Sample 5: Then the witch came off her broomstc. Then the witch went ovr the gobrigh [drawbridge]. Than the witch noct on the door then the princess opind the door then the witch grab the princess and then the witct jragd that princess to her hows. Then a prince so the witch jragen the princss to her hows. Then the prince went aftr the witch bat the prince was to fat. Then the naxt dai the witch jragd the princss to a hi op towr with no stars no dor.

—May of kindergarten[2]

—   Affrication of /t/ or /d/ so that it is changed to /ch/ or /j/:

jragd / **dragged**; *jragen* / **dragging**

—   Use of a single letter for a syllabic consonant /l/, /m/, or /r/:

aftr / **after**; *towr* / **tower**

—   Substitution of vowels that are similar in articulation:

naxt / **next**; *op* / **up**

Sample 6: Apirl hand lenkin worked at the white house.

—End of kindergarten (child lives in Washington, D.C.)

—   Why is this good phonetic spelling for a kindergartener?

Almost all of the speech sounds in the name Abraham Lincoln (*Apirl hand lenkin*) are represented. Phoneme segmentation and working memory are required to do such good approximations.

Chapter 4
Understanding Language Differences

Exercise 4.1: Compare Spanish and English Vowel Phonemes (p. 56)

1. Circle the vowel phonemes in *Figure 4.2* that are not on the Spanish Vowel Phonemes Chart.
    /ĭ/, /ā/, /ă/, /ī/, /ŭ/, /aw/, /o͝o/, /yū/, /ə/, /oi/, /ou/, /er/, /ar/, /or/

2. Which English vowel sounds are likely to be most challenging for a Spanish-speaking learner of English to identify or to pronounce?

    (Same circled vowel sounds as in #1 answer)

3. How could *Figure 4.2* help you explain the English vowel system to a learner of English?

    The figure explicitly defines the vowel system of English and helps
    students learn how each vowel is pronounced in relation to the long
    vowel sounds in Spanish.

Exercise 4.2: Compare Spanish and English Consonant Phonemes (p. 60)

1. Look at the Spanish consonant phonemes in *Figure 4.3* on page 58.

2. Look at the English consonant phonemes in *Figure 4.4* on page 59.

    –   Circle the English consonant phonemes that do not occur in Spanish phonology (i.e., those that are unique to English).
        /d/, /ng/, /v/, /th/, /z/, /sh/, /zh/, /j/, /wh/, /w/, /h/

3. List the English consonant phonemes that a Spanish-speaking learner of English might need extra help in identifying or pronouncing:

    (Same consonant phonemes as in #2 answer)

Take 2 Review (p. 62)

	Spanish-speaking ELLs	**AAVE Speakers**
Phonology (production of speech sounds)	• The sounds /ch/ and /s/ may be substituted for /j/ and /z/. • The short vowels of English may be hard to distinguish because they do not exist in Spanish.	• Sounds in consonant blends may be dropped. • The sound /th/ may be spoken as /d/, /f/, or /v/, depending on its position in a word. • Word endings may be dropped.
Other	• Word order may vary from conventional English patterns. • Students may need a great deal of instruction in basic vocabulary (word meanings).	• Verb forms differ from conventional English, especially auxiliary verbs and forms of the infinitive "to be" (e.g., **am, is, are**).

Chapter 5
Teaching Phonological Skills

Exercise 5.1: View a Video of Teaching Rhyme Production (p. 67)
(No Answer Key. This exercise involves watching a video demonstration.)

Exercise 5.2: Teaching Sound Blending (p. 69)
(No Answer Key. This exercise involves participant role-play.)

Exercise 5.3: View a Video of Teaching Phoneme Segmentation (p. 71)
(No Answer Key. This exercise involves watching a video demonstration.)

Exercise 5.4: View a Video of Teaching Sound Chains (p. 73)
(No Answer Key. This exercise involves watching a video demonstration.)

Exercise 5.5: Minimal Pairs (Advanced) (p. 76)
Sample Answers:

/ē/, /ĭ/ (**eat, it**; **bead, bid**)	/ā/, /ĕ/ (**fail, fell**)	/ĭ/, /ĕ/ (**pin, pen**)
creek, crick; ease, is	"h," etch; mate, met	if, "f"; bid, bed
/ŭ/, /ŏ/ (**bud, bod**)	/ŏ/, /aw/ (**cot, caught**)	/ou/, /oi/ (**plow, ploy**)
nut, not; glum, glom	knotty, naughty	joust, joist; owl, oil
/ch/, /j/ (**rich, ridge**)	/f/, /v/ (**half, have**)	/l/, /r/ (**lock, rock**)*
chain, Jane; batch, badge	fail, veil; safer, saver	flesh, fresh; feel, fear
/y/, /w/ (**yell, well**)		
Yale, wail; yet, wet		

* Note that /r/ after a vowel changes the vowel sound (e.g., **cold** and **cord** no longer have the same vowel sound).

Exercise 5.6: Examine Your Instructional Program (p. 78)
(No Answer Key. Participant answers will vary according to the instructional materials they analyze.)

Chapter 6
Assessment of Phonological Skills

Final Quiz, Module 2 (p. 83)
(Answer Key is in Module 2 Presenter's Kit handouts.)

Index

Note: Page numbers in *italics* refer to the Answer Key.

A

phoneme segmentation
    assessments using, 79
    Identify the Unit of Language, 18, *100*
    for older students, 81
    skills sequences, 20, 22
    for Spanish learners, 60
    View a Video of Teaching Phoneme Segmentation, 71–73
    warm-up task, 6, *98*
phonemes
    affrication, 49, 52, 85, *107*
    allophonic variation, 47–48, 50
    articulation of. *See* articulation
    aspiration, 48
    confusing similar sounds, 27
    consonant. *See* consonants
    defined, 26, 89
    distinguishing between, 27
    examples, 26
    flapping, 49, 51, *107*
    nasalization (nasal sounds), 27, 30, 33, 34, 48–49, 58, 59
    number of, 26
    reasons for learning, 25
    voiced and voiceless, 27, 30, 31, 32, 48, *101*
    vowel. *See* vowels
phonemic awareness. *See* phoneme awareness
phonetic, defined, 8
phonetic spelling, 16
phonics
    alphabetic principle and, 16–17
    defined, 16, 89
    Four-Part Processing Model of Word Recognition, 7
phonological (metalinguistic) awareness (PA), 11–14
    activities, 11, 12, 14
    activities for preschool/beginning kindergarten level, 66–67
    arguments for importance of, 18–19
    defined, 11, 83
    instructional progression for learning (hourglass figure), 11, 13, 17, 65
    teaching. *See* teaching phonological skills
    underdeveloped, confusing words, 27
phonological, defined, 8
phonological memory (PWM), 14–15, 89
phonological patterns
    of African American Vernacular English, 61–62
    of Spanish-speaking learners, 60
phonological processing, 10
    about, 10, 81
    Comprehensive Test of, 80
    defined, 10
    learning new languages and, 26
    phonetics, phoneme awareness, phonics vs., 8
    stimulating, aiding instruction, 64
    weaknesses, 10, 19, 44
phonological processor, 6–7, 15, 18, 26, 46, 54, 89